# SpringerBriefs in Computer Science

*Series Editors*
Stan Zdonik
Peng Ning
Shashi Shekhar
Jonathan Katz
Xindong Wu
Lakhmi C Jain
David Padua
Xuemin Shen
Borko Furht
VS Subrahmanian

For further volumes:
http://www.springer.com/series/10028

Baris M. Kazar • Mete Celik

# Spatial AutoRegression (SAR) Model

## Parameter Estimation Techniques

Baris M. Kazar
Oracle America Inc.
Nashua, NH, USA
baris.kazar@Oracle.com

Mete Celik
Erciyes University
Kayseri, Turkey
mcelik@erciyes.edu.tr

ISSN 2191-5768          e-ISSN 2191-5776
ISBN 978-1-4614-1841-2    e-ISBN 978-1-4614-1842-9
DOI 10.1007/978-1-4614-1842-9
Springer New York Dordrecht Heidelberg London

Library of Congress Control Number: 2012931935

© The Author(s) 2012
All rights reserved. This work may not be translated or copied in whole or in part without the written permission of the publisher (Springer Science+Business Media, LLC, 233 Spring Street, New York, NY 10013, USA), except for brief excerpts in connection with reviews or scholarly analysis. Use in connection with any form of information storage and retrieval, electronic adaptation, computer software, or by similar or dissimilar methodology now known or hereafter developed is forbidden.
The use in this publication of trade names, trademarks, service marks, and similar terms, even if they are not identified as such, is not to be taken as an expression of opinion as to whether or not they are subject to proprietary rights.

Printed on acid-free paper

Springer is part of Springer Science+Business Media (www.springer.com)

*Dedicated*
   *to our advisors Prof. Shashi Shekhar and Prof. David Lilja.*

             *Baris Kazar & Mete Celik*

   *To my wife Neslihan, my teacher parents Mualla Hatice and Kemal, my brothers Ozgur and Caglar, my parent in-laws Fadime and Muzaffer, my brother in-law Emrullah, my sister in-law Emriye, and my whole family.*


                 *Baris Kazar*

   *To my wife Filiz, my son Cagri Fatih, my daughter Elif Huma, my parents Fatma and Metin, and my whole family.*


                 *Mete Celik*

# Acknowledgements

We would like to thank our advisors Professor Shashi Shekhar and Professor David J. Lilja. Without their invaluable help, guidance, and endless support we would never be able to make this study a reality.

We also would like to thank Minnesota Supercomputing Institute (MSI), University of Minnesota Digital Technology Center (DTC) and Army High Performance and Computing Center (AHPCRC), Department of Electrical and Computer Engineering, and Department of Computer Science and Engineering at the University of Minnesota and Department of Computer Engineering at Erciyes University for their financial support and permissions to use their facilities and computing resources.

We are very grateful to the all members of Spatial Database and Spatial Data Mining Group and ARCTiC Labs (Laboratory for Advanced Research in Computing Technology and Compilers) at the University of Minnesota and Birali Runesha and Dr. Shuxia Zhang at the Minnesota Supercomputing Institute for their valuable discussions, critiques, and contributions.

This research also benefited from discussions with many colleagues and friends. We would like to thank Professor Daniel Boley, Professor Pen Chung Yew, Professor Vipin Kumar, Dr. Siva Ravada, Dr. Joshua Yi, Chris Hescott, Dr. Sreekumar Kodakara, Dr. Ying Chen, Dr. Keqiang Wu, Dr. Alex Zhang, Professor Hui Xiong, Professor Sanjay Chawla, Dr. Betsy George, Professor Jin Soung Yoo, Dr. Sangho Kim, Professor Kelley Pace, Professor James P. LeSage, Professor Giannakis Georgios, Professor Resit Sendag, Cetin Yavuz, Professor Vladimir Cherkassky, Professor Paul Schrater, Professor Filiz Dadaser-Celik, Neslihan Erdogan Kazar (MBA), Dr. Shuxia Zhang, and Dr. Birali Runesha for participating in white board discussions, proof reading papers, discussing spatial autoregressive model (SAR) on the phone or on our presentations for hours with great patience, and helping us debugging serial and parallel codes.

# Contents

**1  Introduction** ................................................... 1
   1.1  Background Information ...................................... 2
   1.2  Spatial Data Mining ........................................ 2
   1.3  Related Work .............................................. 3
   1.4  Contributions ............................................. 4
   1.5  Outline and Scope ......................................... 5

**2  Theory behind the SAR Model** ................................. 7
   2.1  Example Neighborhood Matrix (**W**) on Regular (Uniform) Grid
      Space. .................................................... 8
   2.2  Illustration of the Neighborhood Matrix Formation on a 4-by-4
      Regular Grid Space. ....................................... 9
   2.3  Constructing the Neighborhood Matrix **W** on Irregular Grid Space . 11
   2.4  Derivation of the ML (Concentrated Log-likelihood) Function ..... 12
      2.4.1  The Effect of SAR Autoregression Parameter $\rho$ .......... 16
   2.5  Types of Optimization ..................................... 17

**3  Parallel Exact SAR Model Solutions** ........................... 19
   3.1  Problem Statement ........................................ 21
   3.2  The Serial Implementation ................................. 21
   3.3  Proposed Parallel Formulation ............................. 23
      3.3.1  Stage $\mathscr{A}$: Computing Eigenvalues ...................... 24
      3.3.2  Stage $\mathscr{B}$: The Golden Section Search ................. 24
      3.3.3  Stage $\mathscr{C}$: Least Squares ........................... 25
   3.4  Algebraic Cost Model ...................................... 25
   3.5  Experimental Work and Discussion ......................... 29
      3.5.1  Which load-balancing method provides the best speedup? .. 30
      3.5.2  How does problem size impact speedup? ............... 31
      3.5.3  How does chunk size affect speedup? .................. 32
      3.5.4  How does number of processors affect speedup? .......... 32
   3.6  Summary ................................................. 33

**4    Comparing Exact and Approximate SAR Model Solutions** .......... 35
    4.1    Problem Statement  .......................................... 36
    4.2    Approximation by Taylor's Series Expansion  .................. 36
    4.3    Why is Taylor's Series Approximation valid?  ................. 37
    4.4    Approximation by Chebyshev Polynomials ..................... 38
    4.5    Why is Chebyshev Polynomial Approximation valid? ............ 41
    4.6    Experiment Design ........................................... 42
    4.7    Experimental Results ........................................ 42
    4.8    Summary .................................................... 45

**5    Parallel Implementations of Approximate SAR Model Solutions** ..... 47
    5.1    Problem Statement .......................................... 47
    5.2    Related Work ............................................... 48
    5.3    Operation Cost Analysis ..................................... 48
    5.4    Experimental Design ......................................... 49
    5.5    Experimental Results ........................................ 50
    5.6    Summary ................................................... 50

**6    A New Approximation: Gauss-Lanczos Approximated SAR Model
    Solution** .................................................... 51
    6.1    Problem Statement .......................................... 52
    6.2    A New Approximation: Gauss-Lanczos Method ................. 52
    6.3    Algebraic Error Ranking  .................................... 55
    6.4    Experimental Design and System Setup ....................... 55
    6.5    Summary ................................................... 58

**7    Conclusions and Future Work** ................................. 59

**8    Supplementary Materials** ...................................... 61
    8.1    Moran's I Index: Quantifying the Auto-correlation in Datasets ..... 61
    8.2    Simple Overview of Log-likelihood Theory .................... 61
    8.3    Derivation of Log-likelihood Function for SARMA Model ....... 62
    8.4    Proof for Eigen-values of Markov Matrix which are bounded in
           $[-1, +1]$ and occur in $\pm$ pairs ............................... 65
    8.5    Basic Linear Algebra Facts ................................. 67
    8.6    Proof of symmetry of $(\mathbf{I} - \rho\mathbf{W})^T(\mathbf{I} - \mathbf{M})(\mathbf{I} - \rho\mathbf{W})$ ............. 68
    8.7    Proof of $(\mathbf{I} - \rho\mathbf{W})^T(\mathbf{I} - \mathbf{M})(\mathbf{I} - \rho\mathbf{W}) \geq 0$ ..................... 68
    8.8    Single Variable Optimization: The Golden Section Search ........ 69
    8.9    Multi-variable Search ...................................... 70
    References ..................................................... 71

# Chapter 1
# Introduction

Explosive growth in the size of spatial databases has highlighted the need for spatial data analysis and spatial data mining techniques to mine the interesting but implicit spatial patterns within these large databases. Extracting useful and interesting patterns from massive geo-spatial datasets is important for many application domains, such as regional economics, ecology and environmental management, public safety, transportation, public health, business, and travel and tourism [14, 57, 59], because *space is everywhere*. Many classical data mining algorithms, such as linear regression, assume that the learning samples are *independently and identically distributed (i.i.d.)*. This assumption is violated in the case of spatial data due to spatial auto-correlation [2, 57] and in such cases classical linear regression yields a weak model with not only low prediction accuracy [59] but also residual error exhibiting spatial dependence. Modeling spatial dependencies improves overall classification and prediction accuracies.

The spatial autoregression model (SAR) [18, 31, 57] is a generalization of the linear regression model to account for spatial autocorrelation. It has been successfully used to analyze spatial datasets in regional economics and ecology [14, 59]. The model yields better classification and prediction accuracy [14, 59] for many spatial datasets exhibiting strong spatial autocorrelation. However, it is computationally expensive to estimate the parameters of SAR. For example, it can take an hour of computation for a spatial dataset with 10,000 observation points on a single IBM Regatta processor using a 1.3GHz pSeries 690 Power4 architecture with 3.2 GB memory [32, 33]. This has limited the use of SAR to small problems, despite its promise to improve classification and prediction accuracy for larger spatial datasets. For example, SAR was applied to accurately estimate crop parameters [61] using airborne spectral imagery; however, the study was limited to 74 pixels. A second study, reported in [41], was limited to 3888 observation points.

## 1.1  Background Information

The foundations of spatial data mining include spatial statistics and data mining. Spatial statistical models can be divided into three categories: descriptive, explanatory, and predictive models.

Descriptive models characterize the distribution of the spatial phenomenon. Often the description is based on a set of spatial statistics and indices. For example, a spatial distribution may be classified as random or clustered using spatial autocorrelation (e.g., Moran's I coefficient defined in Section 8.1), nearest neighbor index or quadrat analysis [10].

Explanatory models deal with spatial associations, i.e., the relationships between a phenomenon and the factors affecting its spatial distribution. For example, in order to explain why crime clusters occur in a certain area, the roles of population density, density of vacant houses, poverty rates etc. may be examined. More detailed analysis may explore how each factor may influence the crime locations. Example techniques are based on chi-square tests and spatial correlation coefficients using appropriate geographic units.

Predictive models may be used subsequently for prediction or simulation of alternative management strategies. For example, near future crime rates may be predicted given the current conditions and growth factor of significant factors (e.g., population density, poverty rates, education levels) under certain assumptions. Alternatively, these models may explore what may happen if certain conditions are changed via new management strategies. Example techniques include regression using appropriate geographic units, structural factors (e.g., local features of the geographic unit) as well as spatial factors (e.g., absolute location, distance to certain features and neighborhood effects such as spatial autocorrelation).

Spatial modeling may involve all feature types (points, lines, and polygons in both 2 and 3 dimensional geospaces). The choice of geographic unit is a key decision for polygonal features. Polygonal units may be arbitrary (e.g., a grid for regular geometry), based on existing boundaries (e.g., administrative or political), or derived from data distribution (e.g., areas homogeneous with respect to significant factors).

## 1.2  Spatial Data Mining

Spatial data mining, a subfield of data mining, is concerned with the discovery of interesting and useful but implicit knowledge in spatial databases. Common patterns discovered by data mining algorithms include descriptive patterns (e.g., clustering), explanatory patterns (e.g., association rules), and predictive patterns (e.g., classification rules and decision trees). The foundations of data mining algorithms are in statistics and machine learning. One of the goals of data mining algorithms is to scale up to analyze very large datasets which may not fit in the main memory.

Challenges in spatial data mining arise from the following issues. First, classical data mining treats each input as independent of other inputs, whereas spatial patterns often must satisfy the constraints of continuity and high autocorrelation among nearby features. This is also stated by the first law of geography: *Everything is related to everything else but nearby things are more related than distant things.* For example, the population densities of nearby locations are often related. Second, classical data mining deals with numbers and categories. In contrast, spatial data is more complex and includes extended objects such as points, lines, and polygons. Third, classical data mining works with explicit inputs, whereas spatial predicates (e.g., overlap) and attributes (e.g., distance, spatial autocorrelation) are often implicit.

Spatial Data Mining tasks can be classified into four general categories:

- Spatial exception/outlier detection
- Class identification (e.g., spatial classification and clustering)
- Spatial class description (e.g., spatial concept generalization), and
- Dependency detection (e.g., spatial association rules and co-location rules).

The book will focus on one task from the second category, namely the spatial autoregression (SAR) model solutions.

## 1.3  Related Work

SAR model parameters have been estimated using Maximum Likelihood Theory (ML) or Bayesian statistics (Table 1.1). This book focuses on ML-based SAR model solutions.

The ML function (log-likelihood) of the SAR model solution is computed by calculating the minimum of the sum of the logarithm of the determinant (log-det term) of a large matrix and logarithm of the sum-of-squared errors (*SSE*) term [12, 26, 32, 34, 39, 40, 43, 49, 50, 51, 52, 53, 54, 55, 60]. ML-based SAR model solutions can be classified as either exact or approximate, depending on the strategy used to calculate the log-det term of a large matrix (Table 1.1).

In the literature, there are two ML-based exact SAR model solutions, an eigenvalue computation (EV) based solution [40] and a direct (straight) sparse log-det (SLD) based solution [49]. The EV-based approach uses dense data structures to find the determinant of a very large matrix. Because of the dense representation of the matrices in the EV-based approach, LU factorization of a large matrix requires $O(n^3)$ operations, where $n$ is the number of observations. LU factorization is used to compute determinant of the large matrix [20, 23]. This leads to high execution time and memory usage. In the SAR formulation, neighborhood matrix **W** is sparse. Pace and Barry proposed an SLD-based SAR model solution which uses sparse LU factorization using sparse data structures [49]. The number of operations of sparse LU factorization is $O(2nb_ub_l)$, where $b_u$ and $b_l$ correspond to the upper and lower bandwidths of the matrix **W**. Using sparse data structures drastically decreases the computation time and memory usage. However, even if sparse data structures are used, the computation of the computationally expensive log-det term of the log-likelihood

**Table 1.1** Classification of algorithms solving the spatial autoregression model

|  |  | Exact Solutions | Approximate Solutions |
|---|---|---|---|
| Maximum Likelihood | | Applying Direct Sparse Matrix Algorithms [49] | Characteristic Polynomial Approach (Extended version) [26] |
| | | Eigenvalue 1-D Surface Partitioning [40] | Upper and Lower Bounds via Divide and Conquer [52] |
| | | | Taylor Series Approximation [43] |
| | | | ML-based Matrix Exponential Specification [50] |
| | | | Semiparametric Estimates [51] |
| | | | Characteristic Polynomial Approach [60] |
| | | | Graph Theory Approach [55] |
| | | | Spatial Autoregression Local Estimation [53] |
| | | | Gauss-Lanczos Approach [12] |
| | | | Chebyshev Polynomial Approximation [54] |
| | | | Moments of Eigenvalues [46] |
| Bayesian | | None | Bayesian Matrix Exponential Specification [38] |
| | | | Markov Chain Monte Carlo (MCMC) [4, 37] |

function must be repeated in the parameter estimation process of the SAR model. As a result, ML-based exact SAR solutions in the literature exhibit high computational cost and thus are not scalable to large problem sizes.

A Bayesian statistics based SAR model solution is compared with Markov Random Fields (MRF) for binary dependent variables in [59]. The SAR model is implemented using sampling based Markov Chain Monte Carlo (MCMC) method. The general approach of MCMC methods is that when the joint-probability distribution is too complicated to compute analytically, a sufficiently large number of samples from conditional probability distributions is then taken to estimate the statistics of the full joint probability distribution. This is however computationally expensive process with poor convergence properties. It is also a non-trivial task to figure out what priors to choose. MRFs provide a mathematical framework to model the priori knowledge that spatial quantities consist of smooth patches with occasional jumps. The approach in [48] is followed in [59] where it is shown that the maximum a posteriori estimate of a particular configuration of an MRF can be obtained by solving a suitable min-cut multi-way graph partitioning problem.

## 1.4 Contributions

The contributions of this book can be listed as follows:

A parallel formulation for a general exact estimation procedure [31, 32, 33] for SAR model parameters that can be used for spatial datasets embedded in multi-dimensional space is proposed (Chapter 3). The *exact estimation procedure* means that it is the ML (theory) based SAR model parameter estimation with exact log-det computation. In this study, a public domain parallel numerical analysis library is used to implement the steps of the serial solution on an SMP architecture machine, i.e., a single node of an IBM Regatta. To tune the performance, the source code of the library is modified to change parameters such as scheduling and data-partitioning.

Scalable implementations of the SAR model is developed for large geospatial data analysis, characterization of errors between exact and approximate solutions of the SAR model, and experimental comparison of the proposed solutions on real satellite remote sensing imagery having millions of pixels [34] (Chapter 4). Most importantly, this study shows that the SAR model can be efficiently implemented without loss of accuracy, so that large geospatial datasets which are spatially autocorrelated can be analyzed in a reasonable amount of time on general purpose computers with modest memory requirements. An IBM Regatta is used in order to implement parallel versions of the software using open source ScaLAPACK [9] linear algebra libraries. However, the software can also be ported onto general-purpose computers after replacing ScaLAPACK routines with the serial equivalent open source LAPACK [1, 21] routines. Please note that, even though we are using a parallel version of ScaLAPACK, the computational timings presented in the result section are based on serial execution of all SAR model solutions on a single processor.

A parallel version of approximate SAR model solutions are developed using OpenMP and ScaLAPACK in order to reach higher problem size [58] (Chapter 5).

A new ML-based approximate SAR model solution which is called Gauss-Lanczos (GL) approximation is developed (Chapter 6). The results of the prototype implementation in Matlab is presented. The algebraically error ranking of the Chebyshev Polynomial approximation, Taylor's Series expansion approximation and the GL approximation to the solution of SAR model and its variants is presented. In other words, a relationship is established between the error in log-det term, which is the approximated term in the concentrated log-likelihood function and the error in estimating the SAR parameter $\rho$ for all of the approximate SAR model solutions .

## 1.5 Outline and Scope

This book covers ML-based SAR model solutions using dense and/or sparse linear algebra.

The outline is as follows: Chapter 2 introduces the theory of SAR model solution based on ML Theory. Then, a discussion of application of parallel programming techniques to SAR model solution is given in Chapter 3. While Chapter 4 studies the serial approximate SAR model solutions, Chapter 5 discusses the parallel implementation of approximate SAR model solutions. A new relationship between the error in SAR parameter and the error in log-det term as well as a new approximate SAR model solution are presented in Chapter 6. We conclude and summarize the results with a discussion of future work in Chapter 7.

# Chapter 2
# Theory behind the SAR Model

The SAR model [18, 2], also known in the literature as spatial lag model or mixed regressive model, is an extension of the linear regression model and is given in equation (2.1).

$$\mathbf{y} = \rho \mathbf{W} \mathbf{y} + \mathbf{x}\beta + \varepsilon \tag{2.1}$$

The parameters are defined in Table 2.1. The main point to note here is that *spatial autocorrelation* term $\rho \mathbf{W} \mathbf{y}$ is added to the linear regression model in order to model the strength of the spatial dependencies among the elements of the dependent variable, $\mathbf{y}$. One can use Moran's I index (Section 8.1) in order to see whether there is significant spatial dependency in the given dataset (attributes).

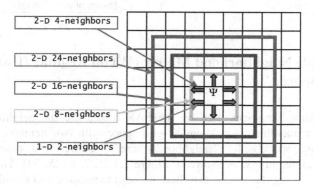

**Fig. 2.1** The neighborhood structures of the pixel on one-dimensional and two-dimensional regular grid space.

**Table 2.1** The notation used in this book

| Variable | Definition | Variable | Definition |
|---|---|---|---|
| $\rho$ | The spatial autoregression (autocorrelation) parameter | $n$ | Problem size (number of observation points or pixels) |
| $y$ | $n$-by-1 vector of observations on the dependent variable | $\beta$ | $k$-by-1 vector of regression coefficients |
| $x$ | $n$-by-$k$ matrix of observations on the explanatory variable | $D$ | $n$-by-$n$ diagonal matrix with elements $\frac{1}{s_i}$, $s_i$ is the row-sum of row i of $C$ |
| $W$ | $n$-by-$n$ neighborhood matrix that accounts for the spatial relationships (dependencies) among the spatial data | $\tilde{W}$ | $n$-by-$n$ symmetric equivalent of $W$ matrix in terms of eigen-values |
| $k$ | Number of features | $|.|$ | Determinant of the "." matrix |
| $\varepsilon$ | $n$-by-1 vector of unobservable error | $(.)^{-1}$ | Inverse of the "." matrix |
| $I$ | Identity matrix | $\sigma^2$ | The common variance of the error $\varepsilon$ |
| $\phi$ | Row dimension of spatial framework (image) | abs | The magnitude of (possibly complex) number |
| $q$ | Column dimension of spatial framework (image) | $\Sigma(.)$ | Summation operation on a matrix/vector |
| $C$ | $n$-by-$n$ binary neighborhood matrix | $\prod$ | Product operation on a matrix/vector |
| $tr(.)$ | Trace of the "." matrix | $\exp(.)$ | Exponential operator i.e., $e^{(.)}$ |
| $\pi$ | Pi constant which is equal to 3.14 | $(.)^T$ | Transpose of the "." matrix/vector |
| $\lambda$ | Eigen-value of a matrix | $(.)_{ij}$ | $ij^{th}$ element of the "." matrix |
| $T_i(.)$ | A Chebyshev polynomial of degree i. "." can be a matrix or a scalar number | $\Sigma$ | $n$-by-$n$ diagonal variance matrix of error defined as $\sigma^2 I$ |
| $N$ | $n$-by-$n$ binary neighborhood matrix from Delaunay triangulation | $O(.)$ | "$O$" notation for complexity analysis of algorithms |
| $q$ | The highest degree of the Chebyshev polynomials | $\Psi$ | Current pixel in the spatial framework (image) with "s" neighbors |
| $\ln(.)$ | Natural logarithm operator | $\cos(.)$ | Cosinus trigonometric operation |
| $k$ | Index variable | $\|.\|_1$ | Norm of the "." matrix |

## 2.1 Example Neighborhood Matrix (W) on Regular (Uniform) Grid Space.

The neighborhood matrices used by the SAR model are the neighborhood relationships on one-dimensional regular grid space with two neighbors and two-dimensional grid space with "s" neighbors, where "s" is four, eight, sixteen, twenty-four and so on neighbors, as shown in Figure 2.1 [5, 7, 8, 25, 34]. This structure is also known as regular square tessellation one-dimensional and two-dimensional planar surface partitioning [25].

## 2.2 Illustration of the Neighborhood Matrix Formation on a 4-by-4 Regular Grid Space

Modeling spatial dependency (or context) improves the overall classification (prediction) accuracy. Spatial dependency can be defined by the relationships among spatially adjacent pixels in a neighborhood within a spatial framework that is a regular grid space. The following paragraph explains how $\mathbf{W}$ in the SAR model is formed. For the four-neighborhood case, the neighbors of the $(i, j)^{th}$ pixel of the regular grid are shown in Figure 2.2.

$$neighbors(i,j) = \begin{cases} (i-1,j) & 2 \geq i \geq \phi, 1 \geq j \geq q \text{ NORTH} \\ (i,j+1) & 1 \geq i \geq \phi, 1 \geq j \geq q-1 \text{ EAST} \\ (i+1,j) & 2 \geq i \geq \phi-1, 1 \geq j \geq q \text{ SOUTH} \\ (i,j-1) & 1 \geq i \geq \phi, 2 \geq j \geq q \text{ WEST} \end{cases}$$

**Fig. 2.2** The four neighbors of the $(i, j)^{th}$ pixel on the regular grid.

The $(i, j)^{th}$ pixel of the surface will fill in the $(\phi * (i-1) + j)^{th}$ row of the non-row-standardized (non-normalized) neighborhood matrix, $\mathbf{C}$. The following entries of $\mathbf{C}$ matrix, i.e. $\{(\phi * (i-1) + j), (\phi * (i-2) + j)\}$, $\{(\phi * (i-1) + j), (\phi * (i-1) + j+1)\}$, $\{(\phi * (i-1) + j), (\phi * (i) + j)\}$ and $\{(\phi * (i-1) + j), (\phi * (i-1) + j-1)\}$ will be "1"s and the others all zeros. The row-standardized neighborhood matrix $\mathbf{W}$ is formed by first finding each row sum (i.e., there will be $\phi \times q$ or $n$ number of row-sums since $\mathbf{W}$ is $\phi \times q$-by-$\phi \times q$) and dividing each element in a row by its corresponding row-sum. In other words, $\mathbf{W} = \mathbf{D}^{-1}\mathbf{C}$ where the elements of the diagonal matrix $\mathbf{D}$ are defined as $d_{ii} = \sum_{i=1}^{n} c_{ij}$ and $d_{ij} = 0$. Figure 2.3 illustrates the spatial framework and the matrices are shown in Figures 2.4(a) and 2.4(b).

| 1 | 2 | 3 | 4 |
|----|----|----|----|
| 5 | 6 | 7 | 8 |
| 9 | 10 | 11 | 12 |
| 13 | 14 | 15 | 16 |

**Fig. 2.3** The spatial framework which is $\phi$-by-$q$ where $\phi$ may or may not be equal to $q$.

The following lemma 2.1 helps in the optimization of the SAR model parameters such that it reduces the search space of the SAR parameter $\rho$.

**Lemma 2.1.** *The eigen-values of the row-stochastic (i.e., row-normalized, row-standardized or Markov) neighborhood matrix $\mathbf{W}$ are in the range $[-1, +1]$ (see also Theorem 5.3 in §2.5 on page 49 of [6]) and occur in $\pm$ pairs.*

**Proof:** Let $\lambda = max_i(\lambda_i)$, and $\lambda_{min} = min_i(\lambda_i)$. By the Perron-Frobenius theorem (please see page 32 of [6] and page 120 of [17]), $\lambda_i \geq -\lambda$. As $\mathbf{W}$ is row-stochastic, we have $\lambda = 1$. This is the first part of the proof. Section 8.4 shows a detailed proof.

$$
\mathbf{C} = \begin{bmatrix}
0 & 1 & 0 & 0 & 1 & 0 & 0 & 0 & 0 & 0 & 0 & 0 & 0 & 0 & 0 & 0 \\
1 & 0 & 1 & 0 & 0 & 1 & 0 & 0 & 0 & 0 & 0 & 0 & 0 & 0 & 0 & 0 \\
0 & 1 & 0 & 1 & 0 & 0 & 1 & 0 & 0 & 0 & 0 & 0 & 0 & 0 & 0 & 0 \\
0 & 0 & 1 & 0 & 0 & 0 & 0 & 1 & 0 & 0 & 0 & 0 & 0 & 0 & 0 & 0 \\
1 & 0 & 0 & 0 & 0 & 1 & 0 & 0 & 1 & 0 & 0 & 0 & 0 & 0 & 0 & 0 \\
0 & 1 & 0 & 0 & 1 & 0 & 1 & 0 & 0 & 1 & 0 & 0 & 0 & 0 & 0 & 0 \\
0 & 0 & 1 & 0 & 0 & 1 & 0 & 1 & 0 & 0 & 1 & 0 & 0 & 0 & 0 & 0 \\
0 & 0 & 0 & 1 & 0 & 0 & 1 & 0 & 0 & 0 & 0 & 1 & 0 & 0 & 0 & 0 \\
0 & 0 & 0 & 0 & 1 & 0 & 0 & 0 & 0 & 1 & 0 & 0 & 1 & 0 & 0 & 0 \\
0 & 0 & 0 & 0 & 0 & 1 & 0 & 0 & 1 & 0 & 1 & 0 & 0 & 1 & 0 & 0 \\
0 & 0 & 0 & 0 & 0 & 0 & 1 & 0 & 0 & 1 & 0 & 1 & 0 & 0 & 1 & 0 \\
0 & 0 & 0 & 0 & 0 & 0 & 0 & 1 & 0 & 0 & 1 & 0 & 0 & 0 & 0 & 1 \\
0 & 0 & 0 & 0 & 0 & 0 & 0 & 0 & 1 & 0 & 0 & 0 & 0 & 1 & 0 & 0 \\
0 & 0 & 0 & 0 & 0 & 0 & 0 & 0 & 0 & 1 & 0 & 0 & 1 & 0 & 1 & 0 \\
0 & 0 & 0 & 0 & 0 & 0 & 0 & 0 & 0 & 0 & 1 & 0 & 0 & 1 & 0 & 1 \\
0 & 0 & 0 & 0 & 0 & 0 & 0 & 0 & 0 & 0 & 0 & 1 & 0 & 0 & 1 & 0
\end{bmatrix}
$$

(a) The non-normalized neighborhood matrix $\mathbf{C}$

$$
\mathbf{W} = \begin{bmatrix}
0 & \frac{1}{2} & 0 & 0 & \frac{1}{2} & 0 & 0 & 0 & 0 & 0 & 0 & 0 & 0 & 0 & 0 & 0 \\
\frac{1}{3} & 0 & \frac{1}{3} & 0 & 0 & \frac{1}{3} & 0 & 0 & 0 & 0 & 0 & 0 & 0 & 0 & 0 & 0 \\
0 & \frac{1}{3} & 0 & \frac{1}{3} & 0 & 0 & \frac{1}{3} & 0 & 0 & 0 & 0 & 0 & 0 & 0 & 0 & 0 \\
0 & 0 & \frac{1}{2} & 0 & 0 & 0 & 0 & \frac{1}{2} & 0 & 0 & 0 & 0 & 0 & 0 & 0 & 0 \\
\frac{1}{3} & 0 & 0 & 0 & 0 & \frac{1}{3} & 0 & 0 & \frac{1}{3} & 0 & 0 & 0 & 0 & 0 & 0 & 0 \\
0 & \frac{1}{4} & 0 & 0 & \frac{1}{4} & 0 & \frac{1}{4} & 0 & 0 & \frac{1}{4} & 0 & 0 & 0 & 0 & 0 & 0 \\
0 & 0 & \frac{1}{4} & 0 & 0 & \frac{1}{4} & 0 & \frac{1}{4} & 0 & 0 & \frac{1}{4} & 0 & 0 & 0 & 0 & 0 \\
0 & 0 & 0 & \frac{1}{3} & 0 & 0 & \frac{1}{3} & 0 & 0 & 0 & 0 & \frac{1}{3} & 0 & 0 & 0 & 0 \\
0 & 0 & 0 & 0 & \frac{1}{3} & 0 & 0 & 0 & 0 & \frac{1}{3} & 0 & 0 & \frac{1}{3} & 0 & 0 & 0 \\
0 & 0 & 0 & 0 & 0 & \frac{1}{4} & 0 & 0 & \frac{1}{4} & 0 & \frac{1}{4} & 0 & 0 & \frac{1}{4} & 0 & 0 \\
0 & 0 & 0 & 0 & 0 & 0 & \frac{1}{4} & 0 & 0 & \frac{1}{4} & 0 & \frac{1}{4} & 0 & 0 & \frac{1}{4} & 0 \\
0 & 0 & 0 & 0 & 0 & 0 & 0 & \frac{1}{3} & 0 & 0 & \frac{1}{3} & 0 & 0 & 0 & 0 & \frac{1}{3} \\
0 & 0 & 0 & 0 & 0 & 0 & 0 & 0 & \frac{1}{2} & 0 & 0 & 0 & 0 & \frac{1}{2} & 0 & 0 \\
0 & 0 & 0 & 0 & 0 & 0 & 0 & 0 & 0 & \frac{1}{3} & 0 & 0 & \frac{1}{3} & 0 & \frac{1}{3} & 0 \\
0 & 0 & 0 & 0 & 0 & 0 & 0 & 0 & 0 & 0 & \frac{1}{3} & 0 & 0 & \frac{1}{3} & 0 & \frac{1}{3} \\
0 & 0 & 0 & 0 & 0 & 0 & 0 & 0 & 0 & 0 & 0 & \frac{1}{2} & 0 & 0 & \frac{1}{2} & 0
\end{bmatrix}
$$

(b) The normalized version i.e., $\mathbf{W}$

**Fig. 2.4** The non-normalized neighborhood matrix $\mathbf{C}$ and the normalized version i.e., $\mathbf{W}$ with 4 nearest neighbors

Now, we deal with the second part of the proof: Since the $\lambda_i$ are real, and all roots of modulus $\lambda$ differ (See page 120 of [17]), there can be at most two $\lambda_i$ of modulus $\lambda$. For sites on a uniform grid such as in Figure 2.1, returns to a site can merely occur after an even number of steps.

In other words, let's consider a symmetric non-row-stochastic matrix like matrix $\mathbf{C}$ or a non-sysmmetric row-stochastic matrix $\mathbf{W}$ derived from the graph as in Figure 2.1 (as suggested by the Perron-Frobenius theorem). First, let's color them as a chess board into two colors such as as red and black as shown in Figure 2.5(a). The neighbors for every red node should be all black, and vice versa. Then, we order all the red nodes first, then all the black nodes are as shown in Figure 2.5(b). Then the corresponding adjacency-like (neighborhood) matrix will look like the structure as shown in Figure 2.5(c) (because no red node is directly connected to another red node, and vice versa.)

As a special case, we have $\mathbf{B} = \mathbf{A}^T$ if binary neighborhood matrix $\mathbf{C}$ is used. It is shown in Figure 2.5(d) where we prove that any matrix of the form shown in Figure 2.5(c) has eigen-values in plus-minus ($\pm$) pairs (except for the zero eigen-values). This means for a row-stochastic $\mathbf{W}$ that all sites have period of two. Thus, $\lambda_{min} = -\lambda_i$ and the eigen-values occur in pairs such as $\pm\lambda_i$. This completes the proof. A similar proof can be found in page 192 of [43] and the first part of this proof can be alternatively found in [6]. $\quad\square$

The rows of $\mathbf{W}$ matrix sum to 1, which means that $\mathbf{W}$ is row-standardized i.e., row-normalized or row-stochastic. A non-zero entry in the $j^{th}$ column of the $i^{th}$ row

| 1R | 2B | 3R | 4B |
|---|---|---|---|
| 5B | 6R | 7B | 8R |
| 9R | 10B | 11R | 12B |
| 13B | 14R | 15B | 16R |

| 1R | 9R | 2B | 10B |
|---|---|---|---|
| 11R | 3R | 12B | 4B |
| 5B | 13B | 6R | 14R |
| 15B | 7B | 16R | 8R |

$$\begin{bmatrix} 0 & A \\ B & 0 \end{bmatrix}$$

(a) The spatial framework visualized as chess-board, which is $\phi$-by-$q$ where $\phi$ may or may not be equal to $q$.

(b) The reordered spatial framework where we gather black nodes and red nodes together.

(c) The corresponding adjacency-like matrix structure

$$\begin{bmatrix} 0 & A \\ B & 0 \end{bmatrix}\begin{bmatrix} u \\ v \end{bmatrix} = \lambda \begin{bmatrix} u \\ v \end{bmatrix} \quad and \quad \begin{bmatrix} 0 & A \\ B & 0 \end{bmatrix}\begin{bmatrix} u \\ -v \end{bmatrix} = -\lambda \begin{bmatrix} u \\ -v \end{bmatrix}$$

(d) Eigen-values of both non-row-stochastic and row-stochastic neighborhood matrices occur in $\pm$ pairs and **u**, **v** are any two vectors

**Fig. 2.5** Proving the lemma 2.1 where B denotes black node and R denotes red node in the grid.

indicates that the $j^{th}$ observation will be used to adjust the prediction of the $i^{th}$ row where $i$ is not equal to $j$.

This section presents forming a **W** matrix for a regular grid with a neighborhood structure that is appropriate for satellite images; however, the **W** matrix can also be formed for irregular (or vector) datasets [25] , which is discussed next.

## 2.3 Constructing the Neighborhood Matrix W on Irregular Grid Space

Spatial statistics requires some means of specifying the spatial dependence among observations [25]. The neighborhood matrix i.e., **W**, spatial weight matrix fulfills this role for lattice models [7, 8] and can be formed on both regular and irregular grid. This section shows a way to form the neighborhood matrix on the irregular grid space which is based on Delaunay triangulation algorithm [52, 53]. [54] describes another method of forming the neighborhood matrix on the irregular grid which is based on nearest neighbors.

One specification of the spatial weight matrix begins by forming the binary adjacency matrix **N** where $N_{ij} = 1$ when observation $j$ is a neighbor to observation $i$ ($i \neq j$). The neighborhood can be defined using computationally very expensive Delaunay triangulation algorithm [36]. These elements may be further weighted to give closer neighbors higher weights and incorporate whatever spatial information the user desires. By itself, **N** is usually asymmetric. To insure symmetry, we can rely on the transformation $\mathbf{C} = (\mathbf{N} + \mathbf{N}^T)/2$. The rest of forming neighborhood matrix on irregular grid follows the same procedure discussed in the proceeding section. Users often re-weight the adjacency matrix to create a row-normalized i.e., row-stochastic matrix or a matrix similar to a row-stochastic matrix. This can be accomplished in the following way:

Let $\mathbf{D}$ represent a diagonal matrix whose $i^{th}$ diagonal entry is the row-sum of the $i^{th}$ row of matrix $\mathbf{C}$. The matrix $\mathbf{W} = \mathbf{D}^{-1/2}\mathbf{D}^{-1/2}\mathbf{C} = \mathbf{D}^{-1}\mathbf{C}$ is row-stochastic where $\mathbf{D}^{-1/2}$ is a diagonal such that its $i^{th}$ entry is the inverse of the square root of the $i^{th}$ row of matrix $\mathbf{C}$. Note that the eigen-values of the matrix $\mathbf{W}$ do not exceed 1 in absolute value as noted in the lemma 2.1, and the maximum eigen-value equals 1 via the properties of row-stochastic matrices (see again the lemma 2.1 in this chapter and §5.13.3 in [42]). Despite the symmetry of $\mathbf{C}$, the matrix $\mathbf{W}$ will be asymmetric in the irregular grid case as well. One can however invoke a similarity transformation for the neighborhood matrices with any number of neighbors as shown in equation 2.2.

$$\tilde{\mathbf{W}} = (\mathbf{D}^{-1/2})^{-1}\mathbf{W}((\mathbf{D}^{-1/2})^{-1})^{-1} = \mathbf{D}^{1/2}\mathbf{W}\mathbf{D}^{-1/2} = \mathbf{D}^{-1/2}\mathbf{C}\mathbf{D}^{-1/2} \qquad (2.2)$$

This results in $\tilde{\mathbf{W}}$ having eigen-values i.e., $\lambda$ equal to those of $\mathbf{W}$ [47]. That is why we call $\tilde{\mathbf{W}}$ the symmetric eigen-value-equivalent matrix of $\mathbf{W}$ matrix. Note that the eigen-values of $\mathbf{W}$ do not exceed 1 in absolute value via the properties of row-stochastic matrices shown in lemma 2.1 in this book and §5.13.3 of [42]) because $\tilde{\mathbf{W}}$ is similar to $\mathbf{W}$ due to the equivalent eigen-values i.e., $-1 \leq \lambda_i^{\tilde{\mathbf{W}}} \leq 1$.

From a statistical perspective, one can view $\mathbf{W}$ as a spatial averaging operator. Given the vector $\mathbf{y}$, the row-stochastic normalization i.e., $\mathbf{W}\mathbf{y}$ results in a form of local average or smoothing of $\mathbf{y}$. In this context, one can view elements in the rows of $\mathbf{W}$ as the coefficients of a linear filter. From a numerical standpoint, the symmetry of $\tilde{\mathbf{W}}$ simplifies computing the logarithm of determinant and has theoretical advantages as well. (See [5, 52, 53, 54] for more information on spatial weight matrices.)

The ML theory estimated SAR model solutions used in this book accepts neighborhood matrices from both regular and irregular grid spaces. The derivation of the ML concentrated log-likelihood function for the SAR model solution, which applies for the SARMA model as shown in Section 8.3, is given in the next section.

## 2.4 Derivation of the ML (Concentrated Log-likelihood) Function

Ordinary least squares are not appropriate to solve for the models described by equation 2.1. One way to solve is to use the ML theory procedure. In probability, there are essentially two classes of problems: the first is to generate a data sample given a probability distribution and the second is to estimate the parameters of a probability distribution given data. Obviously in our case, we are dealing with the latter problem. This derivation not only shows the link between the need for eigen-value computation and the SAR model parameter fitting but also explains how the SAR model works and can be interpreted as an execution trace of the solution for the SAR model. The end-result will be the concentrated log-likelihood function that is used in the optimization of SAR model parameter estimate $\rho$. A simple overview of log-likelihood theory is presented in Section 8.2.

Equation 2.1 can be explicitly written as follows:

$$y_t = (\mathbf{I} - \rho\mathbf{W})^{-1}(x_{t1}\beta_1 + x_{t2}\beta_2 + ... + x_{tk}\beta_k + \varepsilon_t) \tag{2.3}$$

where $t = 1, ..., n$ is the index for $n$ succesive observations. Let us assume that the disturbances or error $\varepsilon_t$ is distributed normally, independently and identically with mean $E(\varepsilon) = 0$ and variance $\sigma^2$. The set of $n$ such equations can be compiled as equation 2.1. Let us assume that the disturbances $\varepsilon_t$, which are the elements of the vector $\varepsilon = [\varepsilon_1, ..., \varepsilon_t, ..., \varepsilon_n]$ and are distributed independently and identically according to a normal distribution defined in equation 2.4. Let's call the matrix $(\mathbf{I} - \rho\mathbf{W})$ as matrix $\mathbf{A}$ to simplify the expressions. Please note that $\varepsilon_t = (\mathbf{A}y_t - x_{t\cdot}\beta)$.

$$N(\varepsilon_t; 0, \sigma^2) = \frac{1}{\sqrt{2\pi\sigma^2}} \exp\left(\frac{-1}{2\sigma^2}(\mathbf{A}y_t - x_{t\cdot}\beta)\right) \tag{2.4}$$

If the vector $\varepsilon$ has a multi-variate normal distribution just like in our case, the normal distribution is then defined in equation 2.5 with a covariance matrix defined as $\Sigma = \sigma^2\mathbf{I}$. Please note that $|\Sigma|^{\frac{-1}{2}} = \sigma^n$, $\Sigma^{-1} = \frac{1}{\sigma^2}\mathbf{I}$ and $|\Sigma| = |\sigma^2\mathbf{I}| = \sigma^{2n}$.

$$N(\varepsilon_t; 0, \Sigma^2) = (2\pi)^{\frac{-n}{2}}|\Sigma|^{\frac{-1}{2}} \exp\left(\frac{-1}{2}\varepsilon_t^T \Sigma^{-1}\varepsilon_t\right)$$

$$= (2\pi)^{\frac{-n}{2}}|\Sigma|^{\frac{-1}{2}} \exp\left(\frac{-1}{2}(\mathbf{A}y_t - x_{t\cdot}\beta)^T \Sigma^{-1}(\mathbf{A}y_t - x_{t\cdot}\beta)\right) \tag{2.5}$$

Then, taking the $x_{t\cdot}$ vectors which forms the rectangular matrix $\mathbf{x}$ of size $n$-by-$k$ as data, the observations $y_t$ (where $t = 1, ..., n$) have density functions $N(y_t; (\mathbf{A}y_t - x_{t\cdot}\beta), \sigma^2)$ which are of the same form as those of the disturbances, and the likelihood function of $\beta$ and $\sigma^2$, based on sample is defined in equation 2.6 [28]. Thus, the prediction of the SAR model solution heavily depends on the quality of the normally distributed random numbers generated.

$$L(\theta|\mathbf{y}) = L((\rho, \beta, \sigma^2)|(y_t, x_{t\cdot}, \mathbf{W})) = \prod_{t=1}^{n} N(y_t; (\mathbf{A}y_t - x_{t\cdot}\beta), \sigma^2)$$

$$= N(\varepsilon; 0, \Sigma^2)|d\varepsilon/dy|$$

$$= (2\pi)^{\frac{-n}{2}}|\Sigma|^{\frac{-1}{2}} \exp\left(\frac{-1}{2}(\mathbf{A}y - \mathbf{x}\beta)^T \Sigma^{-1}(\mathbf{A}y - \mathbf{x}\beta)\right)|d\varepsilon/dy|$$

$$= (2\pi\sigma^2)^{\frac{-n}{2}} \exp\left(\frac{-1}{2}(\mathbf{A}y - \mathbf{x}\beta)^T \Sigma^{-1}(\mathbf{A}y - \mathbf{x}\beta)\right)|d\varepsilon/dy| \tag{2.6}$$

The *Jacobian* term $|d\varepsilon/dy|$ [19, 22] needs to be calculated out in order to find the probability density function of the variable $\mathbf{y}$, which is given by equation 2.7.

Please note that $\varepsilon = (\mathbf{A}\mathbf{y} - \mathbf{x}\beta)$ and the term $\Sigma^{\frac{-1}{2}}(\mathbf{A}\mathbf{y} - \beta)$ is also known as the vector of homoskedastic random disturbances [2, 62]. The Jacobian term is equal to the identity matrix $\mathbf{I}$ in classical linear regression model [2]. The need for the Jacobian term is formally stated and proved by Theorem 7.1 (Theorem 2.1 in this paper) on pages 232-233 of [22]. We provide the theorem and proof for the reader's convenience by converting to our notation.

$$|d\varepsilon/d\mathbf{y}| = |\mathbf{A}| \tag{2.7}$$

**Theorem 2.1.** *Let $N(\varepsilon; 0, \Sigma^2)$ be the value of the probability density of the continuous random variable $\varepsilon$ at $\varepsilon_t$. Since the function given by $\mathbf{y} = \mathbf{A}^{-1}\mathbf{x}\beta + \mathbf{A}^{-1}\varepsilon$ is differentiable and either increasing or decreasing for all values within the range of $\varepsilon$ for which $N(\varepsilon; 0, \Sigma^2) \neq 0$, then for these values of $\varepsilon$, the equation $\mathbf{y} = \mathbf{A}^{-1}\mathbf{x}\beta + \mathbf{A}^{-1}\varepsilon$ can be uniquely solved for $\varepsilon$ to give $\varepsilon = \mathbf{A}\mathbf{y} - \mathbf{x}\beta$ and the probability density of $\mathbf{y}$ is given by:*

$$L(\theta|\mathbf{y}) = N(\varepsilon; 0, \Sigma^2)|d\varepsilon/d\mathbf{y}| \text{ provided } \mathbf{A}^{-1}\mathbf{x}\beta + \mathbf{A}^{-1}\varepsilon \neq 0 \tag{2.8}$$

*Elsewhere, $L(\theta|\mathbf{y}) = 0$.*

**Proof:** The proof can be found on pages 233-235 of [22]. $\square$

$$L(\theta|\mathbf{y}) = (2\pi\sigma^2)^{\frac{-n}{2}} \exp\left(\frac{-1}{2\sigma^2}(\mathbf{A}\mathbf{y} - \mathbf{x}\beta)^T (\mathbf{A}\mathbf{y} - \mathbf{x}\beta)\right) |\mathbf{A}| \tag{2.9}$$

$L(\theta|\mathbf{y})$ shown in equation 2.9 will henceforth be referred to as the "likelihood function of the SAR model". It is a probability distribution but now interpreted as a distribution of parameters which have to be calculated as noted in the Section 8.2. The logarithm of a mutiplication $ABC$ can be written as $\ln(ABC) = \ln(A) + \ln(B) + \ln(C)$. After taking the natural logarithm of equation 2.9, we get the log-likelihood function described by the equation 2.10.

$$\ell(\theta|\mathbf{y}) = \ln L(\theta|\mathbf{y}) = -\frac{n}{2}\ln(2\pi) - \frac{n}{2}\ln(\sigma^2) - $$
$$\frac{1}{2\sigma^2}(\mathbf{A}\mathbf{y} - \mathbf{x}\beta)^T (\mathbf{A}\mathbf{y} - \mathbf{x}\beta) + \ln|\mathbf{A}| \tag{2.10}$$

The MLE estimators in equations 2.11a and 2.11b are obtained by setting $\frac{\partial \ell(\theta|\mathbf{y})}{\partial \beta}$ and $\frac{\partial \ell(\theta|\mathbf{y})}{\partial \sigma^2}$ to zero respectively.

$$\hat{\beta} = (\mathbf{x}^T\mathbf{x})^{-1}\mathbf{x}^T \mathbf{A}\mathbf{y} \tag{2.11a}$$

$$\hat{\sigma}^2 = (\mathbf{A}\mathbf{y})^T (\mathbf{I} - \mathbf{x}(\mathbf{x}^T\mathbf{x})^{-1} \mathbf{x}^T)^T (\mathbf{I} - \mathbf{x}(\mathbf{x}^T\mathbf{x})^{-1} \mathbf{x}^T)(\mathbf{A}\mathbf{y})/n \tag{2.11b}$$

Replacing $\hat{\beta}$ given by equation 2.11a with $\beta$ in equation 2.10 and $\hat{\sigma}^2$ given by equation 2.11b with $\sigma^2$ in equation 2.10 lead to equation 2.12 for the log-likelihood function (i.e. the logarithm of the ML function) to be optimized for $\rho$.

$$\ell(\theta|\mathbf{y}) = \underbrace{\ln|\mathbf{A}|}_{log-det} - \underbrace{\frac{n}{2}\ln(2\pi) - \frac{n}{2}\ln\left\{\frac{1}{n}\right\} - \frac{1}{2n}}_{constants} -$$

$$\frac{n}{2}\ln\underbrace{(\mathbf{Ay})^T(\mathbf{I} - \mathbf{x}(\mathbf{x}^T\mathbf{x})^{-1}\mathbf{x}^T)^T(\mathbf{I} - \mathbf{x}(\mathbf{x}^T\mathbf{x})^{-1}\mathbf{x}^T)(\mathbf{Ay})}_{SSE} \quad (2.12)$$

The first term of equation 2.12, i.e., the log-det, is nothing but the logarithm of the sum of a collection of scalar values including all of the eigen-values of the neighborhood matrix $\mathbf{W}$ as shown by equations 2.13.

$$|\mathbf{I} - \rho\mathbf{W}| = \prod_{i=1}^{n}(1 - \rho\lambda_i) \rightarrow \ln|\mathbf{I} - \rho\mathbf{W}| = \sum_{i=1}^{n}\ln(1 - \rho\lambda_i) \quad (2.13)$$

Hence, equation 2.14 gives the final form of the concentrated log-likelihood function after ignoring constant terms in equation 2.12 and then multiplying the resulting equation with the constant $\frac{-2}{n}$.

$$\min_{|\rho|<1} \frac{-2}{n}\ln|\mathbf{A}| + \ln(\mathbf{Ay})^T(\mathbf{I} - \mathbf{x}(\mathbf{x}^T\mathbf{x})^{-1}\mathbf{x}^T)^T(\mathbf{I} - \mathbf{x}(\mathbf{x}^T\mathbf{x})^{-1}\mathbf{x}^T)(\mathbf{Ay}) \quad (2.14)$$

Therefore, the concentrated log-likelihood function optimized using single-variable optimization routine Golden Section Search to find the best estimates for $\rho$. Once the estimate for $\rho$ is found, both $\beta$ and $\sigma^2$ can be computed. Finally, the predicted variable ($\mathbf{y}$ vectors or thematic classes) can be computed using equation 2.15.

$$\mathbf{y} = (\mathbf{I} - \rho\mathbf{W})^{-1}(\mathbf{x}\beta + \varepsilon) \quad (2.15)$$

Equation 2.15 needs a matrix inversion algorithm in order to get the predicted observed dependent variable ($\mathbf{y}$ vector). For small problem sizes, one can use exact matrix inversion algorithms; however, for large problem sizes (e.g., $> 10,000$) one can use *geometric series expansion* to compute the inverse matrix in equation 2.15 as stated by lemma 2.2.

**Lemma 2.2.**

$$(\mathbf{I} - \rho\mathbf{W})^{-1} = \sum_{i=0}^{\infty}(\rho\mathbf{W})^i$$

**Proof:** Since $\|\mathbf{W}\| \leq 1$ and $|\rho| < 1$, we have that $\|\rho\mathbf{W}\| < 1$. We then apply lemma 2.3.3 on page 58 of [23]. (Please also see page 301 of [29]). $\square$

In practice, we truncate the sum to at most 30 terms, fewer if $\rho$ is bounded away from 1, which results in a very negligible error i.e., error between actual and approximated $\mathbf{y}$ vector is less than an average error of $8.0 \times 10^{-4}\%$.

## 2.4.1 The Effect of SAR Autoregression Parameter ρ

After having presented the problem statement in the previous section, this section illustrates the effect of SAR parameter $\rho$. The plots in Figure 2.6 shows four different cases to illustrate the effect of the SAR parameter $\rho$. These plots aim at showing the smoothing effect of the SAR parameter $\rho$. In (a) and (b) parts of Figure 2.6, there is no Gaussian error so it can be seen there is a symmetric distribution just like the original (i.e., (a)) image. On the other hand the images are disturbed by the Gaussian error in (c) and (d) parts of Figure 2.6. The pixel values in the (bottom) image where $\rho$ is significant increased considerably. Thus, the SAR parameter $\rho$ models the effect of neighbors.

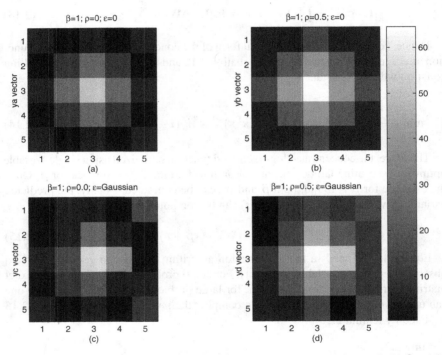

**Fig. 2.6** The sample plots of **x** and **y** vectors (a) $\beta = 1.0$, $\rho = 0$, and the error $\varepsilon = 0$, (b) $\beta = 1.0$, $\rho = 0.5$, and the error $\varepsilon = 0$, (c) $\beta = 1.0$, $\rho = 0$, and the error $\varepsilon$ is normally distributed random numbers, (d) $\beta = 1.0$, $\rho = 0.5$, and the error $\varepsilon$ is normally distributed random numbers.

## 2.5  Types of Optimization

There are two types of optimization. The first type is based on whether we need to use derivative based or non-derivative based search algorithm. The second type is based on whether we should use single variable or multi variable optimization.

*Derivative Based Optimization:* A derivative based optimization that can be used in SAR model solution is Newton-Ralphson (root-finding) algorithm. In this algorithm, we need to compute the first derivative of the log-likelihood function. This gives the location of optimal solution for $\rho$ parameter. The first derivative of log-likelihood function is given by the following equation after expanding the *SSE* term:

$$\frac{\partial \ln L(\mathbf{y})}{\partial \rho} = tr\left((\mathbf{I} - \rho\mathbf{W})^{-1} \frac{\partial(\mathbf{I} - \rho\mathbf{W})}{\partial \rho}\right) - \frac{n}{2}\left(\frac{-\mathbf{y}^T\mathbf{M}^T\mathbf{M}\mathbf{W}\mathbf{y} - \mathbf{y}^T\mathbf{W}^T\mathbf{M}^T\mathbf{M}\mathbf{y} + 2\rho\mathbf{y}^T\mathbf{W}^T\mathbf{M}^T\mathbf{M}\mathbf{W}\mathbf{y}}{\mathbf{y}^T(\mathbf{I} - \rho\mathbf{W})^T\mathbf{M}^T\mathbf{M}(\mathbf{I} - \rho\mathbf{W})\mathbf{y}}\right) \quad (2.16)$$

The first term on the right hand side of equation 2.16 is the derivative of the log-det term with respect to the SAR parameter $\rho$. The term $\mathbf{M}$ corresponds to $[\mathbf{I} - \mathbf{x}(\mathbf{x}^T\mathbf{x})^{-1}\mathbf{x}^T]$. There is problem with this approach such that we need to compute inverse of the large matrix $(\mathbf{I} - \rho\mathbf{W})$. Thus, it is not reasonable to use this approach.

On the other hand, one could use the classical definition of the derivative of a continuous function given in equation 2.17.

**Definition 2.1.** *The First Derivative of A Continuous Function* The first derivative of a continuous function $f(x)$ is given by equation 2.17.

$$\frac{df(x)}{dx} = \frac{f(x + \Delta x) - f(x)}{\Delta x} \quad (2.17)$$

The problem with this approach is that we need to compute two log-dets at each step of the search algorithm according to equation 2.17. Thus, this approach is also costly.

*Single vs. Multi Variable Optimization:* We use Golden Section search which is a one-dimensional search algorithm. We search on the domain of the $\rho$ parameter for SAR model solution. However, we could also use use multi-variable optimization (i.e., quasi-Newton search algorithm) on the $\rho$ and $\beta$ parameters instead of single-variable optimization. Since $\rho$ and $\beta$ parameters are dependent on each other, we preferred single variable optimization. As noted in Section 8.3, the situation is different for the SARMA model where the multi-variable optimization is used because there are two independent parameters to estimate unlike SAR model case.

The problem with only a quadratic cost objective, one part (2.3) of the objective, one of the samples, has the objective equation (2.17) and becomes a cost equation.

$$\min_{u_i, x_i} \frac{1}{2} \sum_{i=0}^{N-1} \left( x_i^T Q x_i + u_i^T R u_i \right)$$

# Chapter 3
# Parallel Exact SAR Model Solutions

The spatial autoregression (SAR) model [18, 31, 57] is a generalization of the linear regression model to account for spatial autocorrelation. It has been successfully used to analyze spatial datasets in regional economics, ecology etc. [14, 59]. The model yields better classification and prediction accuracy for many spatial datasets exhibiting strong spatial autocorrelation.

However, it is computationally expensive to estimate the parameters of the SAR model. For example, it can take an hour of computation for a spatial dataset with 10,000 observation points on an IBM Regatta 32-processor node composed of 1.3GHz pSeries 690 Power4 architecture processors sharing 47.5 GB main memory [32, 33]. This has limited the use of the SAR model to small problems, despite its promise to improve classification and prediction accuracy for larger spatial datasets. Parallel processing is a promising approach to speed-up the sequential solution procedure for the SAR model.

To the best of our knowledge, the only related work [40] implemented the SAR model solution for one-dimensional geo-spaces and used CMSSL [16], a parallel linear algebra library written in CM-Fortran (CMF) for the CM-5 supercomputers of Thinking Machines Corporation, neither of which is available for use anymore. That approach was not useful for spatial datasets embedded in spaces of two or more dimensions. Thus, it is not included in the comparative evaluation in this chapter.

The contributions of this chapter are listed as follows:

1. A parallel formulation for a general exact estimation procedure [25] for SAR model parameters that can be used for spatial datasets embedded in *multi-dimensional space* is proposed. The *exact estimation procedure* means that it is the ML (theory) based SAR model parameter estimation with exact log-det computation. A public domain parallel numerical analysis library is used to implement the steps of the serial solution on an SMP architecture machine, i.e., a single node of an IBM Regatta.
2. To tune the performance, the source code of the library is modified to change parameters such as scheduling and data-partitioning.

3. The algebraic cost model which can be applied to both the serial and the parallel formulations is derived. Thus, this is the first attempt to evaluate the scalability of SAR model solution both analytically and experimentally.

The proposed parallel formulation is evaluated on an IBM Regatta. Results of experiments show that the proposed parallel formulation achieves a speedup of up to 7 on 8 processors within a single node of the IBM Regatta. Different load-balancing techniques supported by OpenMP [13] is compared for improving the speedup of the proposed parallel formulation of the SAR model. Affinity scheduling, which is both a static and dynamic (i.e., quasi-dynamic) load-balancing technique, performs best on average. The impact of other OpenMP parameters, i.e., chunk size defined as the number of iterations per scheduling step is also evaluated. To further improve speedup, an algebraic cost model is developed to characterize the scalability and identify the performance bottlenecks.

Figure 3.1 highlights the three stages of the exact algorithm for the SAR model solution which is based on eigen-value computation. It is based on ML theory, which requires computing the logarithm of the determinant of the large $(\mathbf{I} - \rho\mathbf{W})$ matrix. The first term of the end-result of the derivation of the logarithm of the likelihood function i.e., equation 3.1, clearly shows it is needed to compute the (natural) logarithm of the determinant of a large matrix. In equation 3.1 note that $\mathbf{I}$ denotes an $n$-by-$n$ identity matrix, "$T$" denotes the transpose operator, "ln" denotes the logarithm operator and $\sigma^2$ is the common variance of the error as shown in Table 2.1.

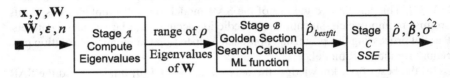

**Fig. 3.1** System diagram of the serial exact algorithm for the SAR model solution

$$\ln L(\mathbf{y}) = \ln|\mathbf{I} - \rho\mathbf{W}| - \frac{n}{2}\ln(2\pi) - \frac{n}{2}\ln\left\{\frac{1}{n}\right\} -$$

$$\frac{n}{2}\underbrace{\ln\left\{\mathbf{y}^T(\mathbf{I} - \rho\mathbf{W})^T\,[\mathbf{I} - \mathbf{x}(\mathbf{x}^T\mathbf{x})^{-1}\mathbf{x}^T]^T\,[\mathbf{I} - \mathbf{x}(\mathbf{x}^T\mathbf{x})^{-1}\mathbf{x}^T](\mathbf{I} - \rho\mathbf{W})\mathbf{y}\right\}}_{SSE} - \frac{1}{2n}$$

$$(3.1)$$

Therefore, Figure 3.1 can be viewed as an implementation of the ML theory. Before describing each stage, next section defines the problem statement.

## 3.1 Problem Statement

Given a spatial framework $S$ for the underlying spatial graph $G$, and attribute functions $f_{\mathbf{x}_k}$ over $S$, and the neighborhood relationship $R$, we can build the SAR model and find its parameters by minimizing the concentrated log-likelihood (objective) function. The problem is formally defined as follows.

*Parallel Scalable (ML Theory Based) Exact SAR Model Solution Problem*
**Given:**

- A spatial framework $S$ consisting of sites $\{s_1, ..., s_{\phi q}\}$ for an underlying geographic space $G$.
- A collection of explanatory functions $f_{\mathbf{x}_k} : S \to R^k$, $k = 1, ..., K$. $R^k$ is the range of possible values for the explanatory functions.
- A dependent function $f_{\mathbf{y}} : R \to R^{\mathbf{y}}$.
- A family $\mathbf{F}$ (i.e., $\mathbf{y} = \mathbf{A}^{-1}\mathbf{x}\beta + \mathbf{A}^{-1}\varepsilon$ where $\mathbf{A} = (\mathbf{I} - \rho\mathbf{W})$) of learning model functions mapping $R^1 \times ... \times R^K \to R^{\mathbf{y}}$.
- A neighborhood relationship on the spatial framework.
- The serial solution described in the Serial Dense Matrix Approach [40]

**Find:** A parallel formulation for multi-dimensional geo-spaces to reduce the response time.

**Objective:** To implement parallel and portable software whose scalability is evaluated analytically and experimentally.

**Constraints:**

- Geographic space $S$ is a multi-dimensional Euclidean Space.
- The values of the explanatory variables $\mathbf{x}$ and the dependent function (observed variable) $\mathbf{y}_{n-by-1}$ may not be independent with respect to those of nearby spatial sites, i.e., spatial autocorrelation exists.
- The domain of explanatory and dependent variables are real numbers.
- The SAR parameter $\rho$ varies in the range $[0, 1)$.
- The error is normally distributed (Gaussian error), i.e., $\varepsilon \sim N(0, \sigma^2 \mathbf{I})$ *IID*. In other words, the error is composed of normally distributed random numbers with unit standard deviation and zero mean.
- The neighborhood matrix $\mathbf{W}$ exhibits sparsity.
- The parallel platform is composed of an IBM Regatta, OpenMP and MPI API's.

## 3.2 The Serial Implementation

Stage $\mathscr{A}$ is composed of three sub-stages: pre-processing, Householder (orthogonal similarity) transformation [23, 56], and QL transformation [15]. The pre-processing sub-stage not only forms the row-standardized (i.e., row-stochastic, row-normalized) neighborhood matrix $\mathbf{W}$, but also converts it to its symmetric eigenvalue-equivalent matrix $\tilde{\mathbf{W}}$. The Householder transformation and QL transformation sub-stages are used to find all of the eigen-values of the neighborhood matrix. The Householder transformation sub-stage takes $\tilde{\mathbf{W}}$ as input and forms the tri-diagonal matrix whose eigen-values are computed by the QL transformation sub-stage. Computing *all* of the eigen-values of the neighborhood matrix takes approximately 99% of the total serial response time, as shown in Table 3.1.

Stage $\mathscr{B}$ computes the best estimate for the SAR parameter $\rho$ for the SAR model. While finding the estimate, the logarithm of the determinant of $(\mathbf{I} - \rho\mathbf{W})$ (log-det term) and the (logarithm of the) *SSE* term need to be computed and summed to get the value of the logarithm of the likelihood (log-likelihood) function at each step of the non-linear one-dimensional parameter optimization. This step uses the Golden Section search [15] (see Section 8.8) and updates the SAR parameter $\rho$ at each step. Other search techniques that are sensitive to derivative of the log-likelihood function (such as running Newton-Ralphson search) on the derivative of the log-likelihood function can also be used. The *SSE* term is computed as $((\mathbf{I} - \mathbf{M})\mathbf{y} - \rho(\mathbf{I} - \mathbf{M})\mathbf{W}\mathbf{y})^2$ where the matrix $\mathbf{M}$ is the symmetric and idempotent matrix $\mathbf{x}(\mathbf{x}^T\mathbf{x})^{-1}\mathbf{x}^T$ (See Section 8.6). If we call the matrix $(\mathbf{I} - \mathbf{M})$ as $\mathbf{K}$ matrix which is also symmetric and idempotent matrix, then the terms $\mathbf{K}\mathbf{y}$ and $\mathbf{K}\mathbf{W}\mathbf{y}$ are precomputed before starting the optimization (or Golden Section search) to save time. These terms are labeled as *constant spatial statistics terms* (please see Figure 3.3). There are three ways to compute the value of the log-likelihood function:

1. Compute the eigen-values of the large dense matrix $\mathbf{W}$ once;
2. Compute the determinant of the large dense matrix $(\mathbf{I} - \rho\mathbf{W})$ at each step of the non-linear optimization;
3. Approximate the log-det term.

For small problem sizes, the first two methods work well; however, for large problem sizes approximate solutions are needed. Equation 2.13 expresses the relationship between the eigen-values of the $\mathbf{W}$ matrix and the logarithm of the determinant of the $(\mathbf{I} - \rho\mathbf{W})$ matrix. The optimization is $O(n)$ complexity. If one wants to use the eigen-value algorithm (applied in this study), it can not find the eigen-values of any dense matrix. Thus, the matrix $\mathbf{W}$ has to be converted to its symmetric version $\tilde{\mathbf{W}}$, whose eigen-values are the same as the original matrix $\mathbf{W}$. The conversion is called *similarity transformation* and shown in lemma 3.1. Figure 3.2 derives the matrix $\tilde{\mathbf{W}}$ from the matrix $\mathbf{C}$.

**Lemma 3.1.** *The similarity transformation which is conversion of the matrix $\mathbf{W}$ into its symmetric version $\tilde{\mathbf{W}}$ both of whose eigen-values are the same is given by:*

$$\tilde{\mathbf{W}} = \mathbf{D}^{-1/2}\mathbf{C}\mathbf{D}^{-1/2} \tag{3.2}$$

*Proof.* The proof for the similarity transformation can be found in p. 311 of [23].

The matrix $\tilde{\mathbf{W}}$ is symmetric and has the same eigen-values as $\mathbf{W}$. The row standardization can be expressed as $\mathbf{W} = \mathbf{D}^{-1}\mathbf{C}$, where $\mathbf{D}$ is a diagonal matrix (Table 2.1). The symmetrization sub-routine is the part of the code that does this job.

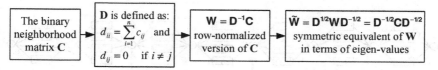

**Fig. 3.2** Derivation of the $\tilde{\mathbf{W}}$ matrix, the symmetric eigen-value equivalent of the $\mathbf{W}$ matrix.

Finally, stage $\mathscr{C}$ computes the optimal sum of the squared error, i.e., *SSE* term to compute the vector of regression coefficients $\beta$ and $\sigma^2$, which is $O(n^2)$ complex. Table 3.1 shows our measurements of the serial response times of the stages of the exact SAR model solution based on ML theory where we compute eigen-values. Each response time given in this study is the average of five runs. As can be seen, computing the eigen-values (stage $\mathscr{A}$) takes a large fraction of the total time.

**Table 3.1** Measured serial response times of stages of the exact SAR model solution for problem sizes of 2,500, 6400 and 10K. Problem size denotes the number of observation points

| Problem Size($n$) | Machine | Serial Execution Time (sec) Spent on | | |
| --- | --- | --- | --- | --- |
| | | Stage $\mathscr{A}$ | Stage $\mathscr{B}$ | Stage $\mathscr{C}$ |
| | | Computing Eigen-values | ML Function | Least Squares |
| 2,500 | SGI Origin | 78.10 | 0.41 | 0.06 |
| | IBM SP | 69.20 | 1.30 | 0.07 |
| | IBM Regatta | 46.90 | 0.58 | 0.06 |
| 6400 | SGI Origin | 1735.41 | 5.06 | 0.51 |
| | IBM SP | 1194.80 | 17.65 | 0.44 |
| | IBM Regatta | 798.70 | 6.19 | 0.42 |
| 10000 | SGI Origin | 6450.90 | 11.20 | 1.22 |
| | IBM SP | 6546.00 | 66.88 | 1.63 |
| | IBM Regatta | 3439.30 | 24.15 | 0.93 |

## 3.3 Proposed Parallel Formulation

The parallel exact SAR model solution implemented in this study use a data-parallelism approach such that each processor works on different data with the same instructions. Data parallelism is chosen since it provides finer granularity for parallelism than functional parallelism as shown in Figure 3.3.

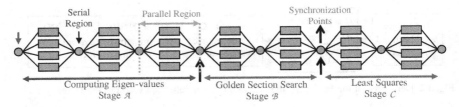

**Fig. 3.3** Data parallelism approach applied to our parallel formulation.

### 3.3.1 Stage 𝒜: Computing Eigenvalues

Stage 𝒜 can be parallelized using parallel eigenvalue solvers [21, 27, 9]. If the source code of the parallel eigenvalue solver is available, the code may be modified in order to tune the performance by changing the parameters such as scheduling technique and chunk size.

A public domain parallel eigenvalue solver from the ScaLAPACK Library [9] is used. This library is available on the MPI-based communication paradigm. Thus, in this study a hybrid programming technique is used to exploit this library within OpenMP, a shared memory programming model which is preferred within each node of the IBM Regatta. The source code of the parallel eigensolver within ScaLAPACK is modified to allow evaluation of different design decisions including the choice of scheduling techniques and chunk sizes. OpenMP provides a rich set of choices for scheduling techniques i.e., static, dynamic, guided, and affinity scheduling techniques. Another important design decision relates to the partitioning of data items. OpenMP and MPI is set to let different processors work on different parts of the neighborhood matrix.

### 3.3.2 Stage 𝐵: The Golden Section Search

The Golden Section search (GSS) needs to compute the logarithm of the maximum-likelihood function for the non-linear optimization (See Section 8.8). The GSS algorithm itself where the non-linear optimization is realized is left un-parallelized since it is very fast in serial format. Parallelization may increase the response time due to the communication overhead. However, the constant (spatial statistics) terms in the ML function are computed in parallel very fast just before starting the non-linear optimization. For instance, it takes only a couple of seconds to compute these constant spatial statistics terms for problem size 10,000 on 8 processors. The serial GSS has linear complexity.

### 3.3.3 Stage $\mathscr{C}$: Least Squares

Once the estimate for the autoregression parameter is computed, the estimate for the regression coefficient $\hat{\beta}$, which is a scalar in our spatial autoregression model, is calculated in parallel. The formula for $\hat{\beta}$ is derived from ML theory. The estimate of the common variance of the error term $\hat{\sigma}^2$ is also computed in parallel to compare with the actual value. The complexity is reduced to $O(n^2/p)$ from $O(n^2)$ due to the parallelization of this stage. The next section computes the algebraic cost model in order to explain the experimental results.

## 3.4 Algebraic Cost Model

This section concentrates on the analysis of the ranking of the load-balancing techniques using the algebraic cost model. First, the notation is introduced in Table 3.2.

**Table 3.2** The notation used in the cost model

| Variable | Definition |
|---|---|
| $t_f$ | Time per flop |
| $t_s$ | Time to prepare a message for transmission (latency) |
| $t_w$ | Time taken by the message to traverse the network to its destination (1/bandwitdh) |
| $n$ | Neighborhood matrix and vector size (problem size) |
| $p$ | Number of processors |
| $B$ | Chunk size |
| $\xi_{static}, \xi_{dynamic}, \xi_{affinity}$ | Load-imbalance factor for static, dynamic and affinity scheduling |
| $T_{prll}$ | Estimated parallel response time |
| $T_{serial}$ | Estimated serial response time |

The algebraic cost model is built in order to explain the experimental results. The cost model consists of two components: computation time and communication time. Before presenting the results of the cost modeling, the load-balancing techniques are introduced that are used in this study to determine the best workload distribution among the processors. These techniques can be grouped in four major classes.

1. Static Load-Balancing (SLB)

   - Contiguous Scheduling: Since $B$ is not specified, the iterations of a loop are divided into chunks of n/p iterations each. This scheduling is referred to as static $B = n/p$.
   - Round-robin Scheduling: The iterations are distributed in chunks of size $B$ in a cyclic fashion. This scheduling is referred to as static $B = \{1, 4, 8, 16\}$.

2. Dynamic Load-Balancing (DLB)

- Dynamic Scheduling: If $B$ is specified, the iterations of a loop are divided into chunks containing $B$ iterations each. If $B$ is not specified, then the chunks consist of $n/p$ iterations. The processors are assigned these chunks on a "first-come, first- do" basis. Chunks of the remaining work are assigned to available processors.
- Guided Scheduling: If $B$ is specified, then the iterations of a loop are divided into progressively smaller chunks until a minimum chunk size of $B$ is reached. The default value for $B$ is 1. The first chunk contains $n/p$ iterations. Subsequent chunks consist of number of remaining iterations divided by $p$ iterations. Available processors are assigned chunks on a "first-come, first-do" basis.

3. Quasi-Dynamic Load-Balancing composed of both static and dynamic components (QDLB)

- Affinity Scheduling: The iterations of a loop are initially divided into $p$ chunks, containing $n/p$ iterations. If $B$ has been specified, then each processor is initially assigned to a chunk, and is then further subdivided into chunks containing $B$ iterations. If $B$ has not been specified, then the chunks consist of half of the number of iterations remaining iterations. When a thread becomes free, it takes the next chunk from its initially assigned partition. If there are no more chunks in that partition, then the thread takes the next available chunk from a partition initially assigned to another thread.

4. Mixed Load-Balancing (MLB):

- Mixed1 and Mixed2 Schedulings: Composed of both static and round-robin scheduling

Our cost model proceeds as follows. In Table 3.2, the time to execute one floating-point operation i.e., a flop is denoted by $t_f$. The serial response time of the SAR model solution is represented by equation 3.3.

$$T_{serial} = 1.33n^3 t_f \qquad (3.3)$$

The time taken to communicate a message between two processors in the network is the sum of $t_s$, the time to prepare a message for transmission, (or; the latency) and $t_w$, the time taken by the message to traverse the network to its destination, (or; the reciprocal of bandwidth). Thus, a single message with m words can be sent from one processor to another processor in time $(t_s + t_w m) \log p$. In the static load-balancing technique, the total parallel response time of the SAR model solution is approximated by a simple expression shown in equation 3.4. Only one communication step of broadcasting is enough to tell each processor what portions of the matrix to process. The matrix is the eigen-value equivalent of the neighborhood matrix i.e., $\tilde{\mathbf{W}}$, and it is in shared-memory so that every processor can read it. These portions are the chunks. Each chunk size is defined by four 4-byte numbers i.e., $(row_{min}, col_{min})$ and $(row_{max}, col_{max})$ at compile-time. The term $\xi_{static}$ is defined as the load-imbalance factor for static scheduling load-balancing technique.

$$T_{prll} = Computation\ Time\ +\ Communication\ Time$$

$$T_{prll} = \frac{T_{serial}}{(1 - \xi_{static}) \times p} + \frac{n}{B} \times (t_s + t_w m) \log p \tag{3.4}$$

In the case of a dynamic load-balancing technique, the total parallel response time can be expressed as in equation 3.5. The term $T_{comm}$ represents the communication overhead for work transfers as shown in equation 3.6 and $\xi_{dynamic}$ is the load-imbalance factor for the dynamic scheduling load balancing technique.

$$T_{prll} = \frac{T_{serial} + T_{comm}}{(1 - \xi_{dynamic})p} + \frac{n}{B} \times (t_s + t_w m) \log p \tag{3.5}$$

$$T_{comm} = (8.5B + 2)\frac{n}{B}t_s + 2.5 \log p \frac{n^2}{\sqrt{p}} t_w \tag{3.6}$$

The total parallel response time for the quasi-dynamic load-balancing technique i.e., affinity scheduling, is the same as equation 3.5 except that the load-imbalance factor is $\xi_{affinity}$. According to our calculations, the communication time is much less than the computation time for all of the total parallel response times. Therefore, we will concentrate on the computation time part of the total parallel response times. As indicated by equations 3.4 and 3.5, the computation time decreases as the number of processors i.e., $p$, increases and as the load-imbalance factor decreases. The load-imbalance factor is lowest for affinity scheduling due to the more uniform distribution of the non-uniform workload where all of the eigen-values of the $\tilde{W}$ matrix are computed. There are two-levels of workload distribution in affinity scheduling. The first one is at compile-time, as in static scheduling, and the second one is at run-time, as in dynamic scheduling. Thus, affinity scheduling benefits from both compile-time and run-time schedulings. As the problem size increases, there will be more work per processor, which leads to better load-balancing. The load-imbalance factor will be highest for the guided scheduling since the first chunk size has $n/p$ iterations, which is similar to static scheduling with chunk size $n/p$. Furthermore, the dynamic chunk distribution overhead will increase the communication cost of guided scheduling more than that of any other load-balancing technique.

Thus, the algebraic cost model reveals that the contiguous and guided scheduling techniques can be categorized as the poorest techniques. The round-robin scheduling technique (static scheduling with chunk sizes $\{1, 4, 8, 16\}$) comes next in the ranking. Figure 3.4 abstracts any parallel program parallelized at the finer granularity level in terms of these two major terms. Here, the main assumption for this cost model is that the time spent in the parallel region is much greater than the time spent in the serial region and $B \ll n/p$, both of which hold for our formulation.

Ignoring the communication cost, we can approximately list the operation counts for the eigen-value based exact SAR model solution in Figure 3.3. The time to execute one floating-point operation i.e., a flop in a rank-$n$ matrix-matrix multiplication of DGEMM and matrix-vector multiplication DGEMV of Scalapack [9] respec-

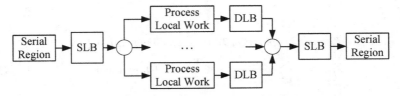

**Fig. 3.4** Generic parallel program parallelized at finer granularity level.

tively are denoted by $\tau_{DGEMM}$ and $\tau_{DGEMV}$. As can be seen, the computation is dominated by the Householder transformation operation.

**Table 3.3** The operation cost for the eigenvalue based exact SAR model solution.

| Tasks in the Eigenvalue Based Exact Sar Model Solution | | Operation Count | |
|---|---|---|---|
| | | Matrix-Martix Mult. (DGEMM) | Matrix-Vector Mult. (DGEMV) |
| Stage $\mathscr{A}$ | Symmetrization | 0 | $n^2 \tau_{DGEMV}$ |
| | Reduction to Tri-diagonal form | $\frac{2}{3}n^3 \tau_{DGEMM}$ | $\frac{2}{3}n^3 \tau_{DGEMV}$ |
| | Bisection | 0 | $120n^2 \tau_{DGEMV}$ |
| | Inverse Iteration | 0 | $400n^2 \tau_{DGEMV}$ |
| Stage $\mathscr{B}$ | Constant spatial stats terms | 0 | $5n^2 \tau_{DGEMV}$ |
| | Golden Section Search | 0 | $n\tau_{DGEMV}$ |
| Stage $\mathscr{C}$ | Least Squares | 0 | $3n\tau_{DGEMV}$ |

Since affinity scheduling does an initial scheduling at compile time, it may have less overhead than dynamic scheduling. The decision tree in Figure 3.5 summarizes a possible total ranking of the load-balancing techniques used in this chapter.

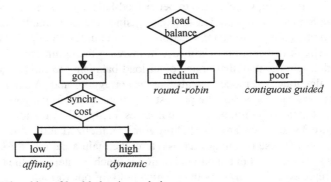

**Fig. 3.5** Total ranking of load-balancing techniques.

## 3.5 Experimental Work and Discussion

Experimental design answers four questions by using synthetic datasets:

1. Which load-balancing method provides best speedup?
2. How does problem size i.e., the number of observation points ($n$), affect speedup?
3. How does chunk size i.e., the number of iterations per scheduling step ($B$), affect speedup?
4. How does number of processors ($p$) affect speedup?

Table 3.4 summarizes the factors and their parameter domains. In the figure, SLB stands for static load-balancing (scheduling) technique, DLB stands for dynamic load-balancing (scheduling) technique, QDLB stands for quasi-dynamic load-balancing (scheduling) technique, and MLB stands for mixed load-balancing (scheduling) technique. The most important factors are load-balancing technique, problem size, chunk size and number of processors. These factors determine the performance of the parallel formulation. 4 neighbors are used in the neighborhood structure, but 8 and more neighbors could also be used. The first response variable is speedup and is defined as the ratio of the serial execution time to the parallel execution time. The second response variable, parallel efficiency, is a metric that is defined as the best speedup number obtained on 8 processors divided by 8. The standard deviation of five runs reported in our experiments for problem size 10,000 is 16% of the average run-time (i.e., 561 seconds). It is 9.5% (i.e., 76 seconds) of the average run-time for problem size 6400 and 10.6% of the average run-time (i.e., 5.2 seconds) for problem size 2,500.

**Table 3.4** Experimental Work

| Factor Name | Parameter Domain | | |
|---|---|---|---|
| Language | f77 w / OpenMP & MPI API's | | |
| Problem Size ($n$) | 2500, 6400, and 1000 observation points | | |
| Neighborhood Structure | 2-D w/ 4- neighbors | | |
| Method | Maximum Likelihood for SAR Model Solution | | |
| Language | f77 w / OpenMP & MPI API's | | |
| Auto-regression Parameter | [0,1) | | |
| Load-balancing | SLB | Contiguous ($B = n/p$ | |
| | | Round-robin w/($B = \{1,4,8,16\}$ | |
| | DLB | Dynamic W/ ($B = \{n/p, 1,4,8,16\}$ | |
| | | Guided w/($B = \{1,4,8,16\}$ | |
| | QDLB | Affinity w/($B = \{n/p, 1,4,8,16\}$ | |
| | MLB | Combined (Contiguous + Round-robin ) | |
| Hardware Platform | IBM Regatta w/ 47.5 GB Main Memory, 32 1.3 GHZ Power4 architecture processors | | |
| Number of Processors | 1, 4, and 8 | | |

### 3.5.1 Which load-balancing method provides the best speedup?

*Experimental Setup*: The response variables are speedup and parallel efficiency. Even though 4 neighbors is used for multi-dimensional geo-spaces, the proposed method can solve for any type of neighborhood matrix structures.

*Trends*: Figure 3.6 summarizes the average speedup results for different load-balancing techniques (i.e. mixed1, mixed2, static w/o $B$, with $B$=(1,4,8,16); dynamic with $B$=(n/p,1,4, 8,16); affinity w/o $B$, with $B$=(1,4,8,16); guided w/o $B$ or with $B = n/p$, and $B$=(4,8,16) for problem sizes ($n$) 10,000, 6400, and 2500 on 1, 4, and 8 processors. Mixed1 scheduling uses static with $B = 4$ (round-robin w/ $B = 4$) for non-uniform workload and static w/o $B$ (contiguous) for uniform workload. Mixed2 scheduling uses static with $B = 16$ (round-robin w/ $B = 16$) for non-uniform work-load and static w/o $B$ (contiguous) for uniform workload. For each problem size, affinity scheduling appears to perform the best. For example, in part (a) of Figure 3.6 affinity scheduling with chunk size 1 provides best speedup. In part (b) of Figure 3.6 for problem size 6,400, affinity scheduling with chunk size 8 provides best speedup. Affinity scheduling with chunk size $n/p$ provides best speedup in part (c) of Figure 3.6 for problem size 2,500. The main reason is that affinity scheduling

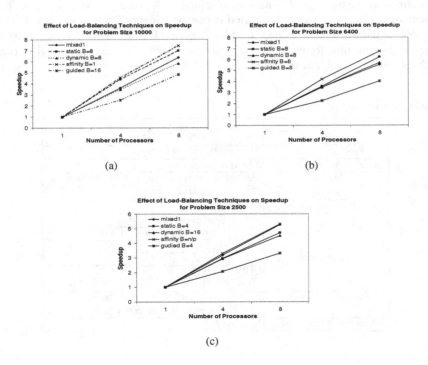

(a)

(b)

(c)

**Fig. 3.6** Effect of load-balancing techniques on speedup on for different problem sizes.

does scheduling both at compile time and run-time, allowing it to adapt quickly to the dynamism in the program without much overhead. Results show that the parallel efficiency increases as the problem size increases. The best parallel efficiency obtained for problem size 10,000 is 93.13%, while for problem size 6,400, it is 83.45%; and for problem size 2,500 it is 66.26%. This is due to the fact that as the problem size increases, the ratio of parallel time spent in the code to the serial time spent also increases.

### 3.5.2 How does problem size impact speedup?

*Experimental Setup*: The number of processors is fixed at 8 processors. The best and worst load-balancing techniques, namely affinity scheduling and guided scheduling, are presented as two extremes. Speedup is the response variable. The chunk sizes and problem sizes are varied. Recall that chunk size is the number of iterations per scheduling step and problem size is the number of observation points.

*Trends*: The two extremes for the load-balancing techniques are shown in Figure 3.7. In the case of affinity scheduling the speedup increases linearly with problem size. In the case of guided scheduling, even though the increase in speedup is not linear as the problem size increases, there is still some speedup. An interesting trend for affinity scheduling with chunk size 1 is that it starts as the worst scheduling but then moves ahead of every other scheduling when the problem size is 10,000 observation points. Since we ran out of memory for problem sizes greater than 10,000 due to the quadratic growth in the **W** matrix, we were unable to observe whether this trend is maintained for larger problem sizes.

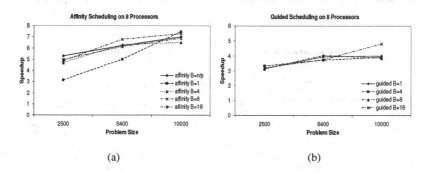

(a)                                                        (b)

**Fig. 3.7** Impact of problem size on speedup using a) affinity and b) guided scheduling on 8 processors.

### 3.5.3 How does chunk size affect speedup?

*Experimental Setup*: The response variable is the speedup. The number of processors is fixed at 8 processors. The problem sizes and the chunk sizes are varied. We want to compare two load-balancing techniques, static scheduling and dynamic scheduling. Static scheduling is arranged only at compile time, while dynamic scheduling is arranged only at run-time.

 *Trends*: Figure 3.8 presents the comparison. As can be seen, there is a value of chunk size between 1 and $n/p$ that results in the highest speedup for each load-balancing scheme. The dynamic scheduling reaches the maximum speedup when chunk size is 16, while static scheduling reaches the maximum speedup at chunk size 8. This is due to the fact that dynamic scheduling needs more work per processor in order to beat the scheduling overhead. There is a critical value of the chunk size for which the speedup reaches the maximum. This value is higher for dynamic scheduling to compensate for the scheduling overhead. The workload is more evenly distributed across processors at the critical chunk size value.

### 3.5.4 How does number of processors affect speedup?

*Experimental Setup*: The chunk size is kept constant at 8 and 16. Speedup is the response variable. The number of processors is varied i.e., $\{4,8\}$. The problem size is fixed at 10,000 observation points.

 *Trends*: As Figure 3.9 shows, the speedup increases as the number of processors goes from 4 to 8. Mixed1 scheduling uses static with $B = 4$ (round-robin w/ $B = 4$) for non-uniform workload and static w/o $B$ (contiguous) for uniform workload. Mixed2 scheduling uses static with $B = 16$ (round-robin w/ $B = 16$) for non-uniform

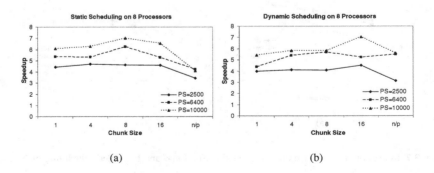

      (a)             (b)

**Fig. 3.8** Effect of chunk size on speedup using a) static and b) dynamic schedulings on 8 processors.

workload and static w/o $B$ (contiguous) for non-uniform workload. The average speedup across all scheduling techniques is 3.43 for the 4-processor case and 5.91 for the 8-processor case. Affinity scheduling shows the best speedup, on average 7 times on 8 processors. Therefore, the speedup increases as the number of processors increases. Guided scheduling results in the worst speedup because the first processor is always assigned a chunk of size $n/p$. The rest of the processors always have less work to do even though the rest of the work can be distributed evenly. The same scenario applies to static scheduling with chunk size $n/p$. Dynamic scheduling tends to result in better speedup as the chunk size increases. However, it also suffers from the same problem of guided and static scheduling techniques when the chunk size is $n/p$. Therefore, it is expected dynamic scheduling will have its best speedup for a chunk size which is somewhere between 16 and $n/p$ iterations.

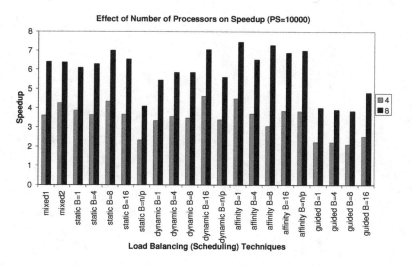

**Fig. 3.9** The effect of number of processors on speedup when problem size is 10000.

## 3.6 Summary

A parallel formulation for a general exact estimation procedure for SAR model parameters that can be used for spatial datasets embedded in multi-dimensional space is developed. Various load-balancing techniques has been studied. The aim was to distribute the workload as uniformly as possible among the processors. The results show that the proposed parallel formulation achieves a speedup up to 7 using 8 processors. The algebraic cost model developed in this study coincides with the experimental work.

# Chapter 4
# Comparing Exact and Approximate SAR Model Solutions

Exact SAR model solution is both memory and compute intensive. It is needed to develop approximate solutions that do not sacrifice accuracy and can handle very large data-sets having billions of observation points. In this chapter, It is proposed to use two different approximations for solving the SAR model solution: Taylor's Series expansion and Chebyshev Polynomials [33]. The purpose of these methods is to approximate the logarithm of the determinant of $(\mathbf{I} - \rho\mathbf{W})$.

This chapter provides the following contributions:

1. Scalable implementations of the SAR model are developed for large geospatial data analysis.
2. The errors between exact and approximate solutions of the SAR model are characterized. The *approximate solution of the SAR model* means that it is again the ML (theory) based SAR model parameter estimation with approximate log-det computation such as Chebyshev Polynomials or Taylor's Series expansion.
3. Experimental comparison of the proposed solutions on real satellite remote sensing imagery having millions of pixels.
4. The theoretical explanation about why approximate methods are appropriate is provided.

An IBM Regatta is uded in order to implement parallel versions of the software using open source ScaLAPACK [9] linear algebra libraries. However, the software can also be ported onto generalpurpose computers after replacing ScaLAPACK routines with the serial equivalent open source LAPACK [1] routines. Please note that, even though we are using a parallel version of ScaLAPACK, the computational timings presented in the results section (please see Table 4.4) are based on serial execution of all SAR model solutions on a single processor. The parallel results are presented in the next chapter.

The remainder of the chapter is organized as follows: Next section presents the problem statement. Next, the approximate SAR model solutions using Taylor's Series expansion and Chebyshev Polynomials are presented and theoretical explanation about why approximate methods are appropriate is given. Then, the experimental design and summary of results are provided.

## 4.1 Problem Statement

The problem studied in this paper is defined as follows:

*Scalable ML Theory Based Approximate SAR Model Solution Problem*

**Given:**

- A spatial framework $S$ consisting of sites $\{s_1, ..., s_{\phi q}\}$ for an underlying geographic space $G$.
- A collection of explanatory functions $f_{\mathbf{x}_k} : S \to R^k$, $k = 1, ..., K$. $R^k$ is the range of possible values for the explanatory functions.
- A dependent function $f_{\mathbf{y}} : R \to R^{\mathbf{y}}$.
- A family $\mathbf{F}$ (i.e., $\mathbf{y} = \mathbf{A}^{-1}\mathbf{x}\beta + \mathbf{A}^{-1}\varepsilon$ where $\mathbf{A} = (\mathbf{I} - \rho \mathbf{W})$) of learning model functions mapping $R^1 \times ... \times R^K \to R^{\mathbf{y}}$.
- A neighborhood relationship on the spatial framework.
- The solution procedure described in the Dense Matrix Approach [40] for one-dimensional geo-spatial datasets.

**Find:** A solution that scales well for large multi-dimensional geo-spatial datasets.
**Objective:** To scalable and portable software for analyzing large geo-spatial datasets.
**Constraints:**

- Geographic space $S$ is a multi-dimensional Euclidean Space.
- The values of the explanatory variables $\mathbf{x}$ and the dependent function (observed variable) $\mathbf{y}_{n-by-1}$ may not be independent with respect to those of nearby spatial sites, i.e., spatial autocorrelation exists.
- The domain of explanatory and dependent variables are real numbers.
- The SAR parameter $\rho$ varies in the range $[0, 1)$.
- The error is normally distributed (Gaussian error), i.e., $\varepsilon \sim N(0, \sigma^2 \mathbf{I})$ *IID*. In other words, the error is composed of normally distributed random numbers with unit standard deviation and zero mean.
- The neighborhood matrix $\mathbf{W}$ exhibits sparsity.

The exact solution still suffers from high computational complexity and memory requirements even in parallel form [32]. These limitations have led us to investigate approximate solutions for the SAR model estimation. In this chapter, two candidate approximate-semi-sparse solutions of the SAR model based on Taylor's Series expansion and Chebyshev Polynomials are developed.

## 4.2 Approximation by Taylor's Series Expansion

[43] suggests an approximation of the log-determinant of a matrix by means of the traces of the powers of the neighborhood matrix, $\mathbf{W}$ (or the symmetric (eigenvalue) equivalent of the neighborhood matrix i.e., $\tilde{\mathbf{W}}$). It basically finds the trace of the matrix logarithm, which is equal to the log-determinant of that matrix. In this approach, the Taylor's Series is used to approximate the function $\sum_{i=1}^{n} \ln(1 - \rho \lambda_i)$

where $\lambda_i$ represents the $i^{th}$ eigen-value that lies in the interval $[-1,+1]$ and $\rho$ is the scalar parameter from the interval $(-1,+1)$. The term $\sum_{i=1}^{n} \ln(1-\rho\lambda_i)$ can be expanded as $\sum_{i=1}^{n} \frac{(\rho\lambda_i)^k}{k}$ provided that $|\rho\lambda_i| < 1$, which will hold for all $i$ if $|\rho| < 1$. Equation 4.1, which states the approximation used for the logarithm of the determinant of the large matrix term of log-likelihood function, is obtained using the relationship between eigen-values and the trace of a matrix, i.e. $\sum_{i=1}^{n} \lambda_i^k = tr(\mathbf{W}^k)$.

$$\ln|\mathbf{I}-\rho\mathbf{W}|^{\frac{-1}{n}} = \frac{1}{n}\sum_{k=1}^{\infty}\left(\frac{tr(\mathbf{W}^k)\rho^k}{k}\right) \tag{4.1}$$

The approximation comes into the picture when we sum up to a finite value, $r$, instead of infinity. Therefore, equation 4.1 is relatively much faster because it eliminates the need to calculate the compute-intensive eigen-value estimation when computing the log-det term. The overall solution is shown in Figure 4.1. The inner structure of Taylors Series expansion is similar to Chebyshev Polynomial except that there is one more vector sum operation which is very cheap to compute. The combination of Taylor's Series approximation, Golden Section search, and *SSE* parts are similar the stages $\mathscr{A}$, $\mathscr{B}$, and $\mathscr{C}$ in Figure 3.1, respectively.

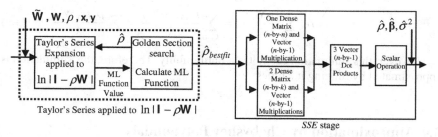

**Fig. 4.1** The system diagram for the Taylor's Series expansion based SAR model solution.

## 4.3 Why is Taylor's Series Approximation valid?

Since $(\mathbf{I}-\rho\mathbf{W})$ is non-singular, there exists a matrix $\omega$ such that $(\mathbf{I}-\rho\mathbf{W})=\exp(\omega)$. This follows from Theorem 6.4.15 (a) of [30]. By taking logarithm of each side of $(\mathbf{I}-\rho\mathbf{W})=\exp(\omega)$, we get $\ln(\mathbf{I}-\rho\mathbf{W})=\omega$ which is substituted in $(\mathbf{I}-\rho\mathbf{W})=\exp(\omega)$ to get $(\mathbf{I}-\rho\mathbf{W})=\exp(\ln(\mathbf{I}-\rho\mathbf{W}))$.

For any square (normal) matrix $\omega$, $|\exp(\omega)|=\exp(tr(\omega))$ where the proof can be found in Problem 6.2.4 of [30] and section 4.14 on page 71 of [42]. The $|.|$ operator denotes determinant of a matrix, "exp" denotes exponential operator and "$tr$" denotes trace of a matrix as noted in Table 2.1.

Thus we have the following:

$$|\mathbf{I} - \rho\mathbf{W}| = |\exp(\ln(\mathbf{I} - \rho\mathbf{W}))| = \exp(tr(\ln(\mathbf{I} - \rho\mathbf{W}))) \qquad (4.2)$$

When the logarithm of both sides of the equation 4.2 is taken, it becomes equation 4.3.

$$\ln|\mathbf{I} - \rho\mathbf{W}| = \ln|\exp(\ln(\mathbf{I} - \rho\mathbf{W}))|$$
$$= \ln\exp(tr(\ln(\mathbf{I} - \rho\mathbf{W}))) = tr(\ln(\mathbf{I} - \rho\mathbf{W})) \qquad (4.3)$$

Using the following property stated in equation 4.4 where the proof can be found on page 566 of [23] and page 492 (i.e., equation 6.5.11) of [30].

$$\ln(\mathbf{I} - \rho\mathbf{W}) = \sum_{k=0}^{\infty} \frac{(\rho\mathbf{W})^k}{k} \ where \ abs(\lambda_{\rho\mathbf{W}}) < 1 \qquad (4.4)$$

Thus, the log-determinant of a matrix becomes computing mainly traces of powers of another matrix as shown in equation 4.5.

$$\ln|\mathbf{I} - \rho\mathbf{W}| = tr(\ln(\mathbf{I} - \rho\mathbf{W}))$$
$$= tr(\sum_{k=0}^{\infty} \frac{(\rho\mathbf{W})^k}{k}) = \sum_{k=0}^{\infty} \frac{tr((\rho\mathbf{W})^k)}{k} = \sum_{k=0}^{\infty} \frac{\rho^k tr(\mathbf{W}^k)}{k} \qquad (4.5)$$

However, this summation can not run until infinity. Therefore, this summation is approximated by running it $r$ times.

## 4.4 Approximation by Chebyshev Polynomials

This approach uses the symmetric equivalent of the neighborhood matrix $\mathbf{W}$ (i.e., $\tilde{\mathbf{W}}$) as in the case of Taylor's Series expansion. The eigen-values of the symmetric matrix $\tilde{\mathbf{W}}$ are the same as those of the neighborhood matrix $\mathbf{W}$. The following lemma 4.1 leads to a very efficient and accurate approximation to the first (log-det) term of the log-likelihood function shown in equation 2.14.

**Lemma 4.1.** *The Chebyshev approximation tries to approximate the logarithm of the determinant of $(\mathbf{I} - \rho\mathbf{W})$ involving a symmetric neighborhood matrix $\tilde{\mathbf{W}}$ as in equation 4.6 which is the relationship of the Chebyshev Polynomials to the logarithm of the determinant of $(\mathbf{I} - \rho\mathbf{W})$ matrix. The three terms are enough for approximating log-det term with an accuracy of 0.03%.*

$$\ln|\mathbf{I} - \rho\mathbf{W}| \equiv \ln|\mathbf{I} - \rho\tilde{\mathbf{W}}| \approx \sum_{j=1}^{q+1} c_j(\rho)tr(T_{j-1}(\tilde{\mathbf{W}})) - \frac{1}{2}c_1(\rho) \qquad (4.6)$$

**Proof:** The next section proves this equality and it is also available in [56]. $\square$

The value of "q" is 3, which is the highest degree of the Chebyshev Polynomials. Therefore, only $T_0(\tilde{\mathbf{W}}))$, $T_1(\tilde{\mathbf{W}}))$, and $T_2(\tilde{\mathbf{W}}))$ have to be computed where:

$$T_0(\tilde{\mathbf{W}})) = \mathbf{I}$$
$$T_1(\tilde{\mathbf{W}})) = \tilde{\mathbf{W}}$$
$$T_2(\tilde{\mathbf{W}})) = 2\tilde{\mathbf{W}}^2 - \mathbf{I}$$
$$... = ...$$
$$T_{k+1}(\tilde{\mathbf{W}})) = 2\tilde{\mathbf{W}}T_{k+1}(\tilde{\mathbf{W}})) - T_{k-1}(\tilde{\mathbf{W}})) \tag{4.7}$$

The Chebyshev Polynomial coefficients $c_j(\rho)$ are given in equation 4.8.

$$c_j(\rho) = \frac{2}{q+1}\sum_{k=1}^{q+1}\ln(1-\rho\cos(\frac{\pi(k-\frac{1}{2})}{q+1}))\cos(\frac{\pi(j-1)(k-\frac{1}{2})}{q+1}) \tag{4.8}$$

In Figure 4.2, the ML function is computed by computing the maximum of the sum of the logarithm of determinant of a large matrix (log-det term) and a least-squares (SSE) term. The SAR parameter $\rho$ that achieves this maximum value is the desired value that makes the classification most accurate. The parameter "q" is the degree of the Chebyshev Polynomials which is used to approximate the term $\ln|\mathbf{I}-\rho\mathbf{W}|$. The pseudocode of the Chebyshev Polynomials approximation is presented in Figure 4.4.1. The following lemma reduces the computational complexity of the Chebyshev Polynomial from $O(n^3)$ to approximately $O(n^2)$.

**Lemma 4.2.** *For regular grid-based nearest-neighbor symmetric neighborhood matrices, the relationship shown in equation 4.9 holds. This relationship saves a tremendous amount of execution time.*

$$tr(\tilde{\mathbf{W}}^2) = \sum_{i=1}^{n}\sum_{i=1}^{n}\tilde{w}_{ij}^2 \text{ where } (i,j)^{th} \text{ element of } \tilde{\mathbf{W}} \text{ is } \tilde{w}_{ij} \tag{4.9}$$

**Proof:** The equality property given in equation 4.9 follows from the symmetry property of the symmetrized neighborhood matrix. In other words, this is valid for all symmetric matrices. The trace operator sums the diagonal elements of the square of the symmetric matrix $\tilde{\mathbf{W}}$. This is the equivalent of saying that the trace operator first multiplies and adds the $i^{th}$ column with the $i^{th}$ row of the symmetric matrix, where the $i^{th}$ column and the $i^{th}$ row of the matrix are the same entries in a symmetric matrix. This results in squaring and summing the elements of the symmetric neighborhood matrix $\tilde{\mathbf{W}}$. Equation 4.9 shows this shortcut for computing the trace of the square of the symmetric neighborhood matrix. $\square$

In Algorithm 4.4.1, the powers of the $\mathbf{W}$ matrices, whose traces are to be computed, go up to 2. The parameter "q" is the degree of the Chebyshev Polynomial which is used to approximate the term $\ln|\mathbf{I}-\rho\mathbf{W}|$. The ML function is computed by calculating the maximum of the log-likelihood functions (i.e. the log-det term plus the *SSE* term). The pseudo-code of the Chebyshev Polynomials approximation approach is presented in Algorithm 4.4.1.

---

**Algorithm 4.4.1:** CHEBYSHEV POLY APPROX TO LOG-DET$(\tilde{\mathbf{W}},n,\hat{\rho},\text{q}=nposs)$

$td1 \leftarrow 0$
$td2 \leftarrow tr(\tilde{\mathbf{W}}^2)$

$cheby-poly-coeffs \leftarrow \begin{bmatrix} 1 & 0 & 0 \\ 0 & 1 & 0 \\ -1 & 0 & 2 \end{bmatrix}$

$nposs \leftarrow 3$

$seq1nposs \leftarrow \begin{bmatrix} 1 \\ 2 \\ 3 \end{bmatrix}$

**for** $k \leftarrow 1$ **to** $nposs$
  **do** $\{xk(k) \leftarrow \cos(\pi(seq1nposs(k)-0.5)/nposs)$
**for** $j \leftarrow 1$ **to** $nposs$

$\quad\text{do}\begin{cases} temp \leftarrow 0 \\ \textbf{for } k \leftarrow 1 \textbf{ to } nposs \\ \quad\text{do}\begin{cases} temp \leftarrow \\ \frac{2}{nposs}\ln(1-\hat{\rho}x_k(k))\cos(\pi(j-1)(seq1nposs(k)-0.5)/nposs) \end{cases} \\ cposs[j] \leftarrow temp \end{cases}$

$tdvec \leftarrow \begin{bmatrix} n \\ td1 \\ td2-0.5n \end{bmatrix}$

$comboterm_{1-by-nposs} \leftarrow cposs_{1-by-nposs} \times cheby-poly-coeffs_{nposs-by-nposs}$
$cheby-logdet-approx_{1-by-1} \leftarrow comboterm_{1-by-nposs} \times tdvec_{nposs-by-1}$
**return** $(cheby-logdet-approx)$

---

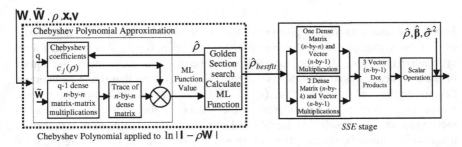

**Fig. 4.2** The system diagram for the Chebyshev Polynomial based SAR model solution.

## 4.5  Why is Chebyshev Polynomial Approximation valid?

As stated in [44], for a better polynomial interpolation of the log-det term i.e., $\ln|\mathbf{I} - \rho\mathbf{W}|$ it is needed to study the Chebyshev Polynomials in the range of $\rho$ parameter i.e., $[-1,+1]$. We proceed from the equation 4.3. Therefore, we approximate $\ln|\mathbf{I} - \rho\mathbf{W}|$ which is equal to $tr(\ln(\mathbf{I} - \rho\mathbf{W}))$ using the Chebyshev Polynomials.

The following theorem 4.1 provides the Chebyshev Polynomial coefficients which will be used to express any function.

**Theorem 4.1.** *If $f(x)$ is an arbitrary function i.e., $\ln(\mathbf{I} - \rho\mathbf{W})$ in the interval $[-1,+1]$, then the N coefficients $c_j$, $j = 1,...,N$, are defined by equation 4.10. Please note that the variable x corresponds to the row-stochastic neighborhood matrix $\tilde{\mathbf{W}}$ and we will apply the trace operation once we get the approximation for the function $\ln(\mathbf{I} - \rho\mathbf{W})$.*

$$
\begin{aligned}
c_j(x) &= \frac{2}{N}\sum_{k=1}^{N} f(x_k)T_{j-1}(x_k) \ \text{(replace function $f$ by $tr(\ln(\mathbf{I}-\rho x))$ and $x$ by $\tilde{\mathbf{W}}$)} \\
&= \frac{2}{N}\sum_{k=1}^{N} f(\cos(\frac{\pi(k-\frac{1}{2})}{N}))\ \cos(\frac{\pi(j-1)(k-\frac{1}{2})}{N} \\
&= \frac{2}{N}\sum_{k=1}^{N} \ln(1 - \rho\cos(\frac{\pi(k-\frac{1}{2})}{N}))\ \cos(\frac{\pi(j-1)(k-\frac{1}{2})}{N}) \quad (4.10)
\end{aligned}
$$

**Proof:** It can be proved using equations (5.8.1), (5.8.4), and (5.8.6) in [56]. $\quad\square$

The equation 4.10 is is the same as equation 4.8 except that we have q + 1 instead of $N$ which arises from truncation that we discuss next. This approximation in equation 4.11, is exact for $x$ equal to all $N$ zeros of $T_N(x)$. Thus, the approximating Chebyshev Polynomial function for $f(x)$ becomes:

$$
f(x) \approx \sum_{k=1}^{N} c_k T_{k-1}(x) - \frac{1}{2}c_1 \quad (4.11)
$$

The fascinating fact [56] about equation 4.11 is that we can *truncate* it to a polynomial of degree q $\ll$ N. The error between the $N^{th}$ degree polynomial and the $q^{th}$ polynomial is dominated by $c_{q+1}T_q(x)$ which is nothing but an oscillatory function with q + 1 equal extrema distributed *smoothly* over the interval $[-1,+1]$ which is a very important property for approximation. By applying the trace operator to the equation 4.11 we get the desired approximate function in equation 4.12 (i.e., also given by equation 4.6), for $tr(\ln(\mathbf{I} - \rho\mathbf{W}))$ which is the same as the log-det term $\ln|\mathbf{I} - \rho\mathbf{W}|$.

$$f(x) \approx \sum_{k=1}^{q+1} c_k tr(T_{k-1}(x)) - \frac{1}{2}c_1 \qquad (4.12)$$

The accuracy of the log-det term approximated by the Chebyshev Polynomials and the Taylor's Series are illustrated in the Tables 4.2 and 4.3.

## 4.6 Experiment Design

The control parameters and experimental setup are summarized in Table 4.1. SAR models have been implemented in Matlab [36]. All solutions have been implemented using a general purpose programming language, f77, and use open source matrix algebra packages (ScaLAPACK [9]).

**Table 4.1** The experimental design

| Factor Name | Parameter Domain |
|---|---|
| Language | f77 |
| Problem Size (n) | 2,500, 10,000 and 2,100,000 observation points |
| Neighborhood Structure | 2-D with 4-neighbors |
| Method | ML Theory Estimation for Exact and Approximate SAR Models |
| Auto-regression Parameter | [0,1) |
| Hardware Platform | IBM Regatta with 1.3 GHz Power4 architecture processor |
| Dataset | Remote Sensing Imagery Data |

## 4.7 Experimental Results

Since the main focus of this study is to find a scalable approximate method for the SAR model solution for very large problem sizes, the first evaluation is to compare the estimates from the approximate methods for the spatial autoregression parameter $\rho$ and the vector of regression coefficients with the estimates obtained from the exact SAR model. Using the percentage error formula, Table 4.2 presents the comparison of accuracies of $\rho$ and $\beta$ obtained from the exact and the approximate (Chebyshev Polynomial and Taylor Series expansion based) SAR model solutions for the 2,500 problem size. The estimates from the approximate methods are very close to the estimates obtained from the exact SAR model solution; there is an error of only 0.57% for the $\rho$ estimate obtained from the Chebyshev Polynomials approxima-tion case and an error of 7.27% for the $\rho$ estimate from the Taylor's Series expansion approximation. A similar situation exists for the $\beta$ estimates. The maximum error among the $\beta$ estimates is 0.7% for the Chebyshev Polynomials approximation case and

8.2for the Taylor's Series expansion approximation. The magnitudes of the errors for the $\rho$ and $\beta$ estimates are on the same order across methods.

**Lemma 4.3.** *Taylor's Series approximation performs worse than Chebyshev Polynomials approximation because Chebyshev Polynomials approximation has a potential error canceling feature of the logarithm of the determinant (log-determinant) of a matrix. Taylor's Series expansion produces different error magnitudes for positive versus negative eigen-value whereas the Chebyshev Polynomials tend to produce error of more equal maximum magnitude [54].*

**Proof:** The main reason behind this phenomenon is that Taylor's Series approximation does better than the Chebyshev Polynomials approximation for values of $\rho$ nearer to zero, bur far worse for extreme (see Sect. 2.3 of [54]). Since the value of $\rho$ is far greater than zero in our case, our experiments also verify this phenomenon, as shown in Table 4.2. ☐

**Table 4.2** The comparison of accuracies of $\rho$ the spatial autoregression parameter, and $\beta$, the vector of regression coefficients or SAR model solutions

| Problem Size($n$) | SAR Model Solution | $\rho$ | $\beta$ | | | | | |
|---|---|---|---|---|---|---|---|---|
| | | | 1 | 2 | 3 | 4 | 5 | 6 |
| | Exact | 0.4729 | -2.473 | -0.516 | 3.167 | 0.0368 | -0.4541 | 3.428 |
| 50x50 (2,500) | Chebyshev | 0.4702 | -2.478 | -0.520 | 3.176 | 0.0368 | -0.456 | 3.440 |
| | Taylor | 0.4385 | -2.527 | -0.562 | 3.291 | 0.0374 | -0.476 | 3.589 |

The second evaluation is to compute the RMS (root-mean-square) error of the estimates of the observed dependent variable ($\mathbf{y}$ vectors or $\hat{\mathbf{y}}$) i.e., the thematic classes. The RMS error is given in equation 4.13a and 4.13b to show how we use it in our formulation. Table 4.3 presents the RMS values for all thematic classes. A representative RMS error value for the Taylor method is 2.0726 and for the Chebyshev method, 0.1686.

$$RMSerror_{cp} = \sqrt[2]{\sum_{i=1}^{n} \left( \frac{(\hat{\mathbf{y}}_{cp} - \hat{\mathbf{y}}_{ee})^2}{n-2} \right)} \tag{4.13a}$$

$$RMSerror_{ts} = \sqrt[2]{\sum_{i=1}^{n} \left( \frac{(\hat{\mathbf{y}}_{ts} - \hat{\mathbf{y}}_{ee})^2}{n-2} \right)} \tag{4.13b}$$

The values of the RMS error suggest that estimates for the observed dependent variable ($\mathbf{y}$ vector or thematic classes) from the Chebyshev Polynomials based SAR model solution are better than those of the Taylor's Series expansion based SAR model solution. This result agrees with the estimates for the spatial autoregression parameter $\rho$ and the vector of regression coefficients $\beta$ shown in Table 4.3.

The predicted images (50 rows by 50 columns) using exact and approximate solutions are shown in Figure 4.3. Although the differences in the images predicted

**Table 4.3** RMS values for each thematic class of a dataset of problem size 2,500

| Training Thematic Class | RMS Error Value for Chebyshev | Taylor | Testing Thematic Class | RMS Error Value for Chebyshev | Taylor |
|---|---|---|---|---|---|
| y1 | 0.1686 | 2.0726 | y1 | 0.1542 | 1.9077 |
| y2 | 0.2945 | 2.0803 | y2 | 0.2762 | 2.0282 |
| y3 | 0.5138 | 3.3870 | y3 | 0.5972 | 4.0806 |
| y4 | 1.0476 | 6.9898 | y4 | 1.4837 | 9.6921 |
| y5 | 0.3934 | 2.4642 | y5 | 0.6322 | 3.9616 |
| y6 | 0.3677 | 2.3251 | y6 | 0.4308 | 2.8299 |
| y7 | 0.2282 | 1.5291 | y7 | 0.2515 | 1.7863 |
| y8 | 0.6311 | 4.3484 | y8 | 0.5927 | 4.0524 |
| y9 | 0.3866 | 3.8509 | y9 | 0.4527 | 4.4866 |

**Table 4.4** The serial execution time in seconds and the memory usage in mega-bytes (MB)

| Problem Size($n$) | Time (Seconds) Exact | Taylor | Chebyshev | Memory (MB) Exact | Taylor | Chebyshev |
|---|---|---|---|---|---|---|
| 50x50 (2,500) | 38 | 0.014 | 0.013 | 50 | 1.0 | 1.0 |
| 100x100 (10,000) | 5100 | 0.117 | 0.116 | 2400 | 4.5 | 4.5 |
| 1200x1800 (2.1M) | Intractable | 17.432 | 17.431 | $\sim 32*10^6$ | 415 | 415 |

by the exact and approximate solutions is hard to notice, there is a huge difference between these methods in terms of computation and memory usage. As can be seen in Table 4.4, even for large problem sizes, the run-times are pretty small due to the fast log-determinant calculation offered by Chebyshev and Taylor's Series approximation. By contrast, with the exact approach, it is impossible to solve any problem having more than $10,000$ observation points. Even if we used sparse matrix determinant computation, it is clear that approximate solutions will still be faster. The approximate solutions also manage to provide close estimates and fast execution times using very little memory. Such fast execution times make it possible to solve solutions for large problems consisting of billions of observation points. The memory usage is very low due to the sparse storage techniques applied to the neighborhood matrix **W**. Sparse techniques cause speedup since the computational complexity of linear algebra operations decrease because of the small number of non-zero elements within the **W** matrix. As seen from Figures 4.1 and 4.2, the most complex operation for Taylor's Series expansion and Chebyshev Polynomial approximated SAR model solutions is the trace of powers of the symmetric neighborhood matrix which requires matrix-matrix multiplications. These operations are reduced to around $O(n^2)$ complexity by Lemma 4.2. All linear algebra matrix operations are efficiently implemented using the ScaLAPACK [9] libraries.

The SAR model is fitted for each observed dependent variable (**y** vector). For each pixel a thematic class label was assigned by taking the maximum of the predicted values. Figure 4.3 shows a set of labeled images for a problem size of 2,500 pixels (50 rows x 50 columns). For a learning (i.e., training) dataset of problem size 2,500, the prediction accuracies of the three methods were similar (59.4% for the exact SAR model, 59.6% for the Chebyshev Polynomials approximated SAR model, and 60.0% for the Taylor's Series expansion approximated SAR model.) We also observed a similar trend on another (testing) dataset of problem size 2,500. The prediction accuracies were 48.32%, 48.4% and 50.4% for the exact solution, Chebyshev Polynomials and Taylor's Series approximation SAR models respectively. This is an interesting result. Even though the estimates for the observed dependent variables ($y$ vectors) or thematic classes are more accurate for the Chebyshev Polynomials based approximate SAR model than for the Taylor's Series expansion approximated SAR model solution, the classification accuracy for the Taylor's Series approximated SAR model solution becomes better than the ones for not only the Chebyshev Polynomials based approximate SAR model but also even the exact SAR model solution. We think that the opposite trend will be observed for larger size images because SAR might need more samples to be trained better. Further research and experimentation is needed to fully understand SAR model's training needs and its impact on prediction accuracy with the solution methods discussed in this chapter.

## 4.8 Summary

One exact and two approximate methods are applied to the SAR model solution using various sizes of remote sensing imagery data i.e., 2,500, 10,000 and 2.1M (2,100,000) observations. The approximate methods applied are Chebyshev Polynomial and Taylor's Series expansion. It is observed that the approximate methods not only consume very little memory but they also execute very fast while providing very accurate results. Although the software is written using a parallel version of ScaLAPACK [9], SAR model solutions presented in this paper can be run either sequentially on a single processor of a node or in parallel on single or multiple nodes. All the results presented in Table 4.4 are based on sequential runs on the same (single) node of an IBM Regetta machine. It should be noted that the software can be easily ported onto general purpose computers and workstations by replacing open source ScaLAPACK routines with the serial equivalent routines in the open source LAPACK [1, 21] library. Currently, LAPACK libraries can be compiled on Windows 98/NT, VAX, and several variants of UNIX.

In this chapter, the focus is on the scalability of the SAR model for large geospatial data analysis using approximate solutions and compared the quality of exact and approximate solutions.

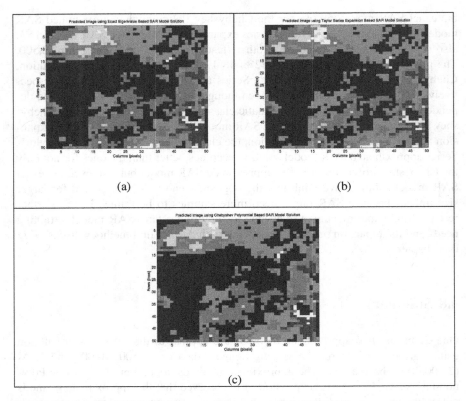

**Fig. 4.3** The images (50x50) using exact and approximate solutions. (a) the image from the exact SAR model solution; (b) the image from the Taylor's Series approximated SAR model solution; (c) the image from the Chebyshev Polynomials approximated SAR model solution.

# Chapter 5
# Parallel Implementations of Approximate SAR Model Solutions

In this chapter, parallel approximate SAR models are developed using hybrid programming and sparse matrix algebra in order to reach very large problem sizes i.e. billions of observations. Hybrid programming enables greater scalability by using MPI across nodes and OpenMP within a single node. The developed parallel approximate SAR model solutions based on Chebyshev Polynomial and Taylor's Series approximations. These solutions can exploit the sparse nature of the neighborhood matrix to save both execution time and memory.

Contributions of this study can be summarized as follows:

1. The proposed parallel solution covers not only single but also multiple-dimensional problems i.e., 2-D, and 3-D geo-spaces for the ML theory based approximate SAR model solution [58].
2. A portable software that can be run on multiple hardware platforms is offered. Any machine specific compiler directives has not been used in order to preserve portability.
3. This is the first attempt to evaluate the scalability of approximate SAR model solution analytically and experimentally.

## 5.1 Problem Statement

First the problem statement and then the operation cost is presented. All of the matrix-vector multiplications in the approximation methods are parallelized in the experiments. The problem studied in this chapter is defined as follows:

*Parallel (ML Theory Based) Approximate SAR Model Solution Problem*
**Given:**

- A spatial framework $S$ consisting of sites $\{s_1, ..., s_{\phi q}\}$ for an underlying geographic space $G$.
- A collection of explanatory functions $f_{\mathbf{x}_k} : S \rightarrow R^k$, $k = 1, ..., K$. $R^k$ is the range of possible values for the explanatory functions.

- A dependent function $f_{\mathbf{y}} : R \to R^{\mathbf{y}}$.
- A family $\mathbf{F}$ (i.e., $\mathbf{y} = \mathbf{A}^{-1}\mathbf{x}\beta + \mathbf{A}^{-1}\varepsilon$ where $\mathbf{A} = (\mathbf{I} - \rho\mathbf{W})$) of learning model functions mapping $R^1 \times \ldots \times R^K \to R^{\mathbf{y}}$.
- A neighborhood relationship on the spatial framework.
- The solution procedure described in the Dense Matrix Approach [40] for one-dimensional geo-spatial datasets.

**Find:** A parallel solution of approximade SAR model.
**Objective:** To scalable and portable software for analyzing large geo-spatial datasets.
**Constraints:**

- Geographic space $S$ is a multi-dimensional Euclidean Space.
- The values of the explanatory variables $\mathbf{x}$ and the dependent function (observed variable) $\mathbf{y}_{n-by-1}$ may not be independent with respect to those of nearby spatial sites, i.e., spatial autocorrelation exists.
- The domain of explanatory and dependent variables are real numbers.
- The SAR parameter $\rho$ varies in the range $[0, 1)$.
- The error is normally distributed (Gaussian error), i.e., $\varepsilon \sim N(0, \sigma^2 \mathbf{I})$ *IID*. In other words, the error is composed of normally distributed random numbers with unit standard deviation and zero mean.
- The neighborhood matrix $\mathbf{W}$ exhibits sparsity.

## 5.2 Related Work

To the best of our knowledge, there is only one other parallel implementation of the spatial autoregression model solution, which is in one-dimension. The approach tries to solve by finding all of the eigen-values of a dense symmetric neighborhood matrix i.e., $\mathbf{W}$ for regular square tessellation one-dimensional planar surface partitioning. However, this parallel formulation used parallelized versions of the eigen-value subroutines from CMSSL, a parallel linear algebra library written in CM-Fortran (CMF) for the CM-5 supercomputers of Thinking Machines Corporation, neither of which is available for use anymore. Thus, it can be stated that the parallel formulation presented in this study is the only parallel spatial autoregression formulation available in the literature. Furthermore, the spatial autoregression model solution presented here is more generic, harder to solve, and covers not only single but also multi-dimensional geo-spaces as well.

## 5.3 Operation Cost Analysis

Ignoring the communication cost, the operation counts can approximately be listed for the Chebyshev Polynomial (and also Taylor's Series expansion) approximated

SAR model solution in Figure 5.1. Affinity scheduling is applied because of its uniform load-balancing characteristics as discussed in Chapter 3. The time to execute one floating-point operation i.e., a flop in a rank-$n$ matrix-matrix multiplication of DGEMM and matrix-vector multiplication DGEMV of Scalapack [9] respectively are denoted by $\tau_{DGEMM}$ and $\tau_{DGEMV}$. The variable $p$ corresponds to the number of processors. Chebyshev Polynomials and Taylor's Series approximations are dominated by the matrix-vector multiplication operations. There are a couple of very tall-thin matrix small matrix multiplications which are decomposed into matrix-vector multiplications in the cost model. Because tall-thin matrix small matrix multiplication operation is not really a matrix-matrix multiplication. As can be seen in Figure 5.1, the computation cost is very low with respect to exact SAR model solutions.

| Tasks in the Chebyshev Poly Approximated SAR Model Solution | | Computation Costs | | Communication Costs | |
|---|---|---|---|---|---|
| | | Matrix-Matrix Mult. (DGEMM) | Matrix-Vector Mult. (DGEMV) | Latency | Bandwodth$^{-1}$ |
| Stage A | Symmetrization (Serial) | 0 | $n^2\tau_{DGEMV}$ | 0 | 0 |
| Stage B | Constant spatial stats terms | 0 | $5\dfrac{n^2}{p}\tau_{DGEMV}$ | $(8.5n+2p)\tau_{lat}$ | $4\dfrac{n^2}{p}\tau_{band}$ |
| | Chebyshev Polynomial (Serial) | 0 | $\sim 10\tau_{DGEMV}$ | 0 | 0 |
| | Golden Section Search (Serial) | 0 | $n\tau_{DGEMV}$ | 0 | 0 |
| Stage C | Least Squares | 0 | $3\dfrac{n^2}{p}\tau_{DGEMV}$ | $(8.5n+2p)\tau_{lat}$ | $4\dfrac{n^2}{p}\tau_{band}$ |

**Fig. 5.1** The operation cost for the Chebyshev Polynomial (and also Taylor's Series expansion) approximated SAR model solution.

## 5.4 Experimental Design

The control parameters for our experiments are summarized in Table 5.1. All the experiments were carried out using the experimental setup summarized in Table 5.1.

**Table 5.1** The experimental design

| Factor Name | Parameter Domain |
|---|---|
| Problem Size ($n$) | 2,500, 6,400, 10,000 observation points |
| Neighborhood Structure and Matrix | 2-D with 4-neighbors |
| Candidates | Chebyshev Polynomials Approximate SAR model solution |
| SAR Parameter $\rho$ | [0,1) |
| Dataset | Remote Sensing Imagery Data |
| Number of Processors | $p = 2, 4, 8$ on a single node of IBM Regatta |

## 5.5 Experimental Results

Figure 5.2(a) shows the serial and parallel execution times (in seconds) of computing the logarithm of the determinant of a matrix in the SAR model solution using Chebyshev approximation. Computing all of the eigen-values of the neighborhood matrix, which is used to compute the logarithm of the determinant of a matrix, takes approximately 99% of the total serial response time [31, 32, 34] and up to an hour to compute a 10,000 problem size. By contrast, as shown in the Figure 5.2(a), it takes only slightly more than 16 seconds to solve the same problem size using Chebyshev polynomial approximation. Chebyshev approximation thus not only scales much better than the eigen-value based approach in terms of execution time but also uses very little memory [34]. Figure 5.2(b) shows the parallel execution times of the Chebyshev Polynomial approximated log-det computation for the problem size 10,000 while varying the number of processors $p$ as 2,4 and 8. Both figures successfully demonstrate the scalability of approximate SAR model solutions.

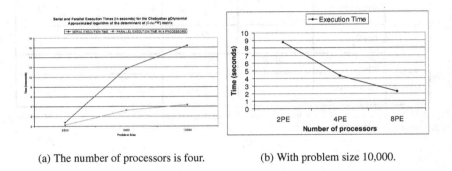

(a) The number of processors is four.            (b) With problem size 10,000.

**Fig. 5.2** The parallel execution times (in seconds) for the Chebyshev polynomial approximated logarithm of the determinant of matrix

## 5.6 Summary

We applied parallel processing techniques to two approximate methods for the SAR model solution using various sizes of remote sensing imagery data i.e., 2,500, 6,400 and 10,000 observations. Incorporating the autocorrelation term in the SAR model enables better prediction accuracy with respect to linear regression. However, computational complexity increases due to the logarithm of the determinant of a large matrix. In order to reach very large dataset sizes, we developed scalable approximate SAR model solutions in this study.

# Chapter 6
# A New Approximation: Gauss-Lanczos Approximated SAR Model Solution

In this chapter, a new approximate ML theory based solution for the SAR model which is called Gauss-Lanczos (GL) approximation is developed. The key idea of the proposed algorithm is to find only the some of the eigenvalues of a large matrix, instead of finding all the eigenvalues, by reducing the size of large matrix dramatically using GL algorithm [3]. Because of this property of GL algorithm, we can save huge computation costs, especially when the matrix size is quite large. The performance comparisons of the proposed method is compared with the other approximate solution methods, which were studied in the previous chapter namely Taylor's Series expansion approximation and Chebyshev Polynomials approximation, by using algebraic error ranking. In contrast to the related approximate SAR model solutions, proposed GL algorithm provides better approximation when the data is strongly correlated (i.e., spatial dependency is high) and problem size gets high. The use of algebraic error ranking revealed a novel relationship between the error in the log-det term, which is the approximated term in the concentrated log-likelihood function and the error in estimating the SAR parameter $\rho$ for all of the approximate SAR model solutions. According to the analysis we can estimate the error on the SAR model parameter $\rho$ using the error on the logarithm of the determinant (log-det) term.

Major contributions of this chapter include the following:

1. A new ML theory based approximate SAR model solution and its variants is developed. The new approximation solution is called GL approximation and we present the results of the prototype in this chapter.
2. The Lanczos algorithm is used for tri-diagonalization (i.e., bandwidth reduction) of the $(\mathbf{I} - \rho \tilde{\mathbf{W}}) \equiv (\mathbf{I} - \rho \mathbf{W})$ matrix.
3. The GL algorithm is used for eliminating computation of some of the eigenvalues of the $(\mathbf{I} - \rho \tilde{\mathbf{W}}) \equiv (\mathbf{I} - \rho \mathbf{W})$ matrix.
4. The error of the Chebyshev Polynomial approximation, Taylor's Series approximation and the GL approximation is algebraically ranked to the solution of the SAR model and its variants. In other words, a relationship is established between the error in log-det term, which is the approximated term in the concentrated log-

likelihood function and the error in estimating the SAR parameter $\rho$ for all of the approximate SAR model solutions.

This chapter covers serial formulations for sparse-approximate solutions to the SAR model and develops a new approximation technique for the SAR model solution. The next section presents the problem statement for this chapter.

## 6.1 Problem Statement

The problem studied in this paper is defined as follows:

*Algebraic Error Ranking of (ML Theory Based) Approximate SAR Model Solution Problem*

**Given:**

- A spatial framework $S$ consisting of sites $\{s_1, ..., s_{\phi q}\}$ for an underlying geographic space $G$.
- A collection of explanatory functions $f_{\mathbf{x}_k} : S \to R^k$, $k = 1, ..., K$. $R^k$ is the range of possible values for the explanatory functions.
- A dependent function $f_{\mathbf{y}} : R \to R^{\mathbf{y}}$.
- A family $\mathbf{F}$ (i.e., $\mathbf{y} = \mathbf{A}^{-1}\mathbf{x}\beta + \mathbf{A}^{-1}\varepsilon$ where $\mathbf{A} = (\mathbf{I} - \rho\mathbf{W})$) of learning model functions mapping $R^1 \times ... \times R^K \to R^{\mathbf{y}}$.
- A neighborhood relationship on the spatial framework.
- The solution procedure described in the Dense Matrix Approach [40] for one-dimensional geo-spatial datasets.

**Find:** A solution that scales well for large multi-dimensional geo-spatial datasets.
**Objective:** To develop scalable SAR methods for analyzing large geo-spatial datasets.
**Constraints:**

- Geographic space $S$ is a multi-dimensional Euclidean Space.
- The values of the explanatory variables $\mathbf{x}$ and the dependent function (observed variable) $\mathbf{y}_{n-by-1}$ may not be independent with respect to those of nearby spatial sites, i.e., spatial autocorrelation exists.
- The domain of explanatory and dependent variables are real numbers.
- The SAR parameter $\rho$ varies in the range $[0, 1)$.
- The error is normally distributed (Gaussian error), i.e., $\varepsilon \sim N(0, \sigma^2 \mathbf{I})$ *IID*. In other words, the error is composed of normally distributed random numbers with unit standard deviation and zero mean.
- The neighborhood matrix $\mathbf{W}$ exhibits sparsity.

## 6.2 A New Approximation: Gauss-Lanczos Method

The GL method was introduced by [3]. In [3], the eigen-value problems are converted to the problem of computing a quadratic form $u^T f(A)u$ (in our case $A$ equals the symmetric positive definite matrix $(ln|\mathbf{I} - \rho\mathbf{W}|))$ where $A$ is a matrix, $u$ is a vector and $f$ is a function. Then the authors convert the problem of computing the quadratic form to a Riemann-Stieltjes integral problem, and then use Gauss-type quadrature rules to approximate the integral. For the approximation, orthogonal polynomial theory and Lanczos procedure are used.

$$\ln|\mathbf{I} - \rho\mathbf{W}| \equiv \ln|\mathbf{I} - \rho\tilde{\mathbf{W}}| = tr(\ln(\mathbf{I} - \rho\mathbf{W})) = tr(\ln\mathbf{A}) \approx \frac{1}{m}\sum_{i=1}^{m} I_r^{(i)} \quad (6.1)$$

In equation 6.1 the quadrature formula is represented by $I_r$. In [3], the GL method proposed to calculate the $I_r$. (Please see the pseudo-code in Figure 6.1 and equation 4.4). The eigen-values of $T_r$ are the nodes. The eigen-vectors of $T_r$ are already normalized. The system diagram of the GL approximation is presented in Figure 6.2.

$$I_r = \sum_{k=1}^{r} w_k^2 f(\lambda_k) \quad (6.2)$$

In equation 6.2, $f(\lambda_k)$ term is used to calculate eigen-values of the matrix $\mathbf{W}$.

$$f(\lambda_k) = \frac{(\lambda_i - x_{j-1}^T(\mathbf{I} - \rho\mathbf{W})x_{j-1})p_{j-1}(\lambda_i) - \gamma_{i-1}p_{j-2}(\lambda_i)}{\| (\mathbf{I} - \rho\mathbf{W})x_{j-1} - (x_{j-1}^T(\mathbf{I} - \rho\mathbf{W})x_{j-1})x_{j-1} - \gamma_{i-1}x_{j-1} \|_2} \quad (6.3)$$

The $w_k$ term of the equation 6.2 is the squares of the first element of the normalized eigen-vectors of $\mathbf{W}$. [45] gives the analytical formulations to calculate the eigen-vectors of real symmetric tri-diagonal matrices. In this study, these formulations are used to calculate the first element $(w_k)$ of the normalized eigen-vector of the $T_r$ matrix.

$$w_k = s_1 s_2 \prod_{i=3}^{r-1} s_i \quad (6.4)$$

where

$$s_1 = \frac{|b_1|}{[b_1^2 + (a_1 - \lambda_k)^2]^{1/2}}$$

$$c_1 = (\lambda_k - a_1)s_1 b_1$$

$$s_2 = \frac{|b_2|}{b_2^2 + [b_1 s_1 + (a_2 - \lambda_k)c_1]^{2^{1/2}}}$$

$$c_2 = \frac{[(\lambda_k - a_2)c_1 - b_1 s_1]s_2}{b_2}$$

$$s_i = \frac{|b_i|}{(b_i^2 + [(\lambda_k - a_i)c_{i-1} - b_{i-1}s_{i-1}c_{i-2}]^2)^{1/2}}$$

$$c_i = [(\lambda_k - a_i)c_{i-1} - b_{i-1}s_{i-1}c_{i-2}]s_i/b_i \tag{6.5}$$

The index $i$ runs from 3 to $r - 1$ equation 6.5.

---

**Algorithm 6.2.1:** GL APPROX($\mathbf{W}, \mathbf{A} = (\mathbf{I} - \rho\tilde{\mathbf{W}}), n, m, r$)

$x_0 \leftarrow 0$
$x_{-1} \leftarrow 0$
$\gamma_0 \leftarrow 0$
**for** $j \leftarrow 1$ **to** $r$

**do** $\begin{cases} a_j \leftarrow x_{j-1}^T A x_{j-1} \\ v_j \leftarrow A x_{j-1} - a_j x_{j-1} - \gamma_{j-1} x_{j-2} \\ \gamma_j \leftarrow \| v_j \|_2 \\ x_j \leftarrow v_j/\gamma_j \end{cases}$

*Compute eigen − values* $\lambda_k$ *of* $T_r$
*Compute first elements* $w_k$ *of eigen − vectors of* $T_r$
*Compute* $I_r$
**return** $(I_r)$

---

**Fig. 6.1** The pseudo-code of the GL algorithm. We repeat this algorithm $m$ times independently to get an average of the ensemble of $I_r$ values.

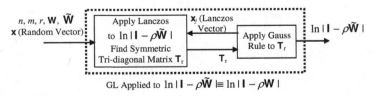

**Fig. 6.2** System diagram of GL Approximated SAR Model Solution

This section ends by illustrating the accuracy of the log-det term approximated by Chebyshev polynomials and the Taylor's series in Figures 6.3 and 6.4.

## 6.3 Algebraic Error Ranking

We formulate the relative error ranking of the approximations to log-det and hence the effect on the estimation of the SAR parameter $\rho$.

We can say that $\rho = f^{-1}(\ell(\theta|\mathbf{y}))$. Thus the change (error) in the concentrated log-likelihood due to the approximation is reflected in the estimation of the parameter $\rho$ as follows where the operator $\triangle$ denotes the difference between the exact (i.e., true) and the approximated values:

$$\triangle \rho_1 = \frac{df^{-1}(\ell(\theta|\mathbf{y}))}{d\ell(\theta|\mathbf{y})} \triangle \ell_1(\theta|\mathbf{y}) \tag{6.6}$$

$$\triangle \rho_2 = \frac{df^{-1}(\ell(\theta|\mathbf{y}))}{d\ell(\theta|\mathbf{y})} \triangle \ell_2(\theta|\mathbf{y}) \tag{6.7}$$

The quantity $\triangle \rho_\#$ is the error in $\rho$ obtained from the approximate method. The quantity $\triangle \ell_\#(\theta|\mathbf{y})$ is the error in the concentrated log-likelihood function from the approximate method, which we can compute algebraically. Since we have the same *SSE* term for all SAR model solutions as we do not approximate it (i.e., $\triangle SSE = 0$), the term $\triangle \ell_\#(\theta|\mathbf{y})$ corresponds directly to the error in the log-det approximation i.e., $\triangle \ln|\mathbf{I} - \rho \mathbf{W}|$.

## 6.4 Experimental Design and System Setup

In the experiments synthetic datasets were generated for different problem sizes, such as $n = 400, 1600, 2500$ and for different spatial auto-regression parameters. We took 4-neighbors (i.e., North, South, East, and West neighbors) of the interested cell (location) and all experiments were run on the same platform. All the experiments were carried out using the same experimental setup summarized in Table 6.1. The system setup of the experiments is shown in Figure 6.2.

ML-based solutions of the SAR require computing the log-det of a large matrix $(\mathbf{I} - \rho \mathbf{W})$, which is computationally expensive. Approximate SAR model solutions try to approximate the log-det of a large matrix by reducing computation cost of this term. It is observed that exact SAR model solution takes approximately 2 orders of magnitude of more time than approximate solutions. In this chapter, ML-based approximate SAR model solutions are algebraically ranked .

In the experiments, the behavior of the candidate algorithms is evaluated for different problem sizes and for different spatial autocorrelation values. Exact and approximated results for the log-det term of the SAR model are given in Figure 6.3 and 6.4. The results of the GL approximation are the average of several runs. Synthetic datasets are generated for different $\rho$ parameters. Figure 6.3 shows the approximation results for the log-det term of the SAR model of the candidate methods. The experiments are ran for three different problem sizes, such as 400, 1600,

**Table 6.1** The experimental design

| Factor Name | Parameter Domain |
|---|---|
| Problem Size ($n$) | 400, 2,500, 6,400 observation points |
| Neighborhood Structure | 2-D with 4-neighbors |
| Candidates | Exact (Eigen-value Computation Based) Approach |
| | Taylor's Series Approximated Approach |
| | Chebyshev Polynomial Approximated Approach |
| | Gauss-Lanczos (GL) Approximated Approach |
| SAR Parameter $\rho$ | $[0,1)$ |
| Chebyshev and Taylor parameters | q=2 |
| | Upper and Lower bounds for Taylor |
| GL parameters | $m = 100 * r$ |
| | Random Number: $\pm 1$ with probability 50% |
| Dataset | Regular Grid $\mathbf{W}$ and $\tilde{\mathbf{W}}$ Matrices |

and 2500. It is observed that Taylor's series approximation gives upper and lower bounds of the approximation log-det term of the SAR model for all problem sizes. Chebyshev approximation gives the optimum results when the spatial autocorrelation parameter $\rho$ is close to zero for all problem sizes. In contrast, for all problem sizes, GL approximation gives better results than Chebyshev approximation when the autocorrelation is high such as spatial autocorrelation parameter is close to 1. This behavior of the GL approximation can be explained by the fact that many cancellations occur while the GL calculates the logarithms of all the eigenvalues of matrix $T_r$ when the spatial autocorrelation low ($\rho$ is close to zero).

Figure 6.4 gives the difference in the accuracy of the results by approximation methods where the difference in the accuracy is defined by the absolute relative error defined in equation 6.8. It is observed that absolute relative error (% accuracy) of Taylor's series and Chebyshev approximations increase while $\rho$ parameter is increasing but Chebyshev approximation gives better results than Taylor's series approximation. In contrast, absolute relative error of GL algorithm decreases while $\rho$ parameter is increasing. GL algorithm gives more accurate results than the other methods. Therefore, GL is better than the other candidate solutions when the spatial autocorrelation is high ($\rho$ is close to 1).

$$\text{Difference in Accuracy} = 100 \times abs \left( \frac{\ln|\mathbf{I} - \rho\mathbf{W}|_{exact} - \ln|\mathbf{I} - \rho\ \mathbf{W}|_{approximated}}{\ln|\mathbf{I} - \rho\mathbf{W}|_{exact}} \right)$$
$$(6.8)$$

The computational cost of the Chebyshev approximation is $O(n^3)$. The cost of the Chebyshev approximation can be reduced to approximately $O(n^2)$. In contrast, the cost of the GL approximation is $2mrO(n^2)$, which includes $2mr$ matrix-vector multiplications of the rank-n matrix. Thus, GL is slightly more expensive than Chebyshev and Taylor's series approximations. In the GL procedure, m represents the number of iterations. In the experiments, m was fixed (i.e., m=400) for each problem size. If the problem size is large enough, the effect of m will be less in the computation

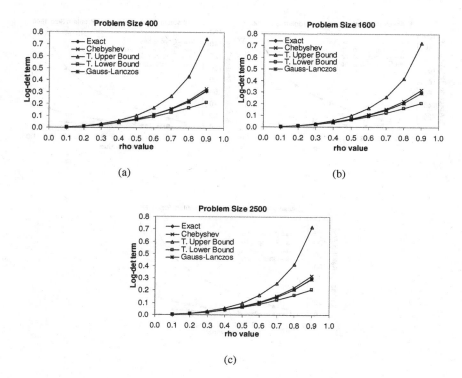

**Fig. 6.3** Exact and approximate values of log-det of SAR model

cost. In GL, r represents the size of tri-diagonal symmetric matrix $\mathbf{T}$ where $r \ll n$. The size of the $\mathbf{T}$ matrix changes during the GL procedure according to various the problem sizes and parameters. In the experiments the value of $r$ varies between 5 and 8 where $r \ll n$ for problem sizes 400, 1600, 2500. The effect of the $r$ parameter will also be less for the larger problem sizes. Results show that GL approximation is one of the candidate solutions for large problem sizes, especially when the spatial autocorrelation is high, and $m$ and $r$ parameters are smaller than the problem size.

It is also observed that the quality of the results of the GL algorithm depends on the number of iterations, as discussed before, and the initial Lanczos vector which is selected randomly. In the experiments, the initial Lanczos vector is selected as a discrete random vector where values of components are either -1 or 1 with the probability of 0.5. Finally, it is also observed that increasing the number of iterations can decrease the effect of the random number generator. However, increasing the number of iterations may lead to the increase in the computation cost of the GL approximation.

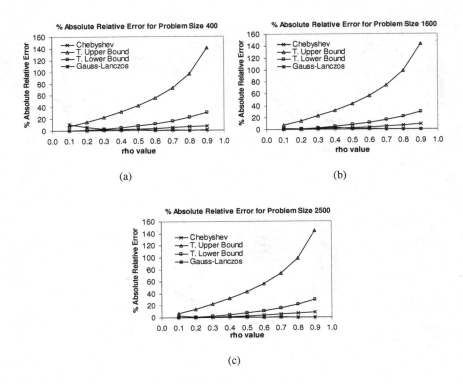

**Fig. 6.4** % absolute relative errors of approximation methods defined in equation 6.4

## 6.5 Summary

A new ML theory based approximate SAR model solution and its variants is developed. The new approximation solution is called Gauss-Lanczos (GL) approximation and we present the results of the prototype in this chapter.

The error of the Chebyshev Polynomial approximation, Taylor series approximation and the GL approximation to the solution of the SAR model and its variants is algebraically ranked. In other words, a relationship is established between the error in log-det term, which is the approximated term in the concentrated log-likelihood function and the error in estimating the SAR parameter $\rho$ for all of the approximate SAR model solutions.

# Chapter 7
# Conclusions and Future Work

Linear regression is one of the best-known classical data mining techniques. However, it makes the assumption of independent identical distribution (*i.i.d.*) in learning data samples, which does not work well for geo-spatial data, which is often characterized by spatial autocorrelation. In the SAR model, spatial dependencies within data are taken care of by the autocorrelation term, and the linear regression model thus becomes a spatial autoregression model. Incorporating the autocorrelation term enables better prediction accuracy. However, computational complexity increases due to the need for computing the log-det of a large matrix $(\mathbf{I} - \rho\mathbf{W})$, which is computed either directly or by finding all of the eigen-values of the $\mathbf{W}$ matrix.

The contributions of this book can be listed as follows:

1. A parallel formulation for a general exact estimation procedure [31, 32, 33] is developed for SAR model parameters that can be used for spatial datasets embedded in multi-dimensional space is proposed (Chapter 3). Various load-balancing techniques has been studied. The aim was to distribute the workload as uniformly as possible among the processors. The results show that the proposed parallel formulation achieves a speedup up to 7 using 8 processors. The algebraic cost model developed in this study coincides with the experimental work.

2. Scalable implementations of the SAR model is developed for large geospatial data analysis, characterization of errors between exact and approximate solutions of the SAR model, and experimental comparison of the proposed solutions on real satellite remote sensing imagery having millions of pixels [34] (Chapter 4). Most importantly, this study shows that the SAR model can be efficiently implemented without loss of accuracy, so that large geospatial datasets which are spatially autocorrelated can be analyzed in a reasonable amount of time on general purpose computers with modest memory requirements.

3. A parallel version of approximate SAR model solutions are developed using OpenMP and ScaLAPACK in order to reach higher problem size [58] (Chapter 5).

4. A new ML-based approximate SAR model solution which is called Gauss-Lanczos (GL) approximation is developed (Chapter 6). The results of the pro-

totype implementation in Matlab is presented. The algebraic error ranking of the Chebyshev Polynomial approximation, Taylor's Series expansion approximation and the GL approximation to the solution of SAR model and its variants is presented. In other words, a relationship is established between the error in log-det term, which is the approximated term in the concentrated log-likelihood function and the error in estimating the SAR parameter $\rho$ for all of the approximate SAR model solutions.

A few future work ideas are listed below:

1. Multi-variable optimization can be applied on both the SAR parameter $\rho$ and the regression coefficient vector $\beta$.
2. Derivative sensitive (Newton-Ralphson) search based optimization can be used. It can help further reduce the number of times log-det term is computed, which in turn will reduce the number of iterations during the optimization process.
3. The upper bound for Taylor's series can be investigated. It is quite larger than the true value of log-det term compared to its lower bound.
4. Bayesian statistics based SAR model solution i.e., Markov Chain Monte Carlo (i.e., MCMC) approximation can be compared with the Maximum Likelihood Theory based approaches.
5. Ways of expressing the spatial dependency using wavelets can be investigated.

# Chapter 8
# Supplementary Materials

This section includes the supplementary materials that are mentioned in this book.

## 8.1 Moran's I Index: Quantifying the Auto-correlation in Datasets

Spatial autocorrelation analysis tests whether the observed value of a variable at one locality is independent of the values of the variable at neighbouring localities. If a dependence exists, the variable is said to exhibit spatial autocorrelation. Spatial autocorrelation measures the level of interdependence between the variables, and the nature and strength of that interdependence. It may be classified as either positive or negative. In a positive case all similar values appear together, while a negative spatial autocorrelation has dissimilar values appearing in close association [35].

$$I = \frac{n}{S_0} * \frac{\sum_{i=1}^{n} \sum_{j=1}^{n} (w_{ij} * (x_i - \bar{x}) * (x_j - \bar{x}))}{\sum_{i=1}^{n} (x_i - \bar{x})^2} \tag{8.1}$$

The term $S_0$ is equal to $\sum_{i=1}^{n} \sum_{j=1}^{n} w_{ij}$ and $n$ is the problem size.

## 8.2 Simple Overview of Log-likelihood Theory

Let $\mathbf{Y} = (Y_1, Y_2, ..., Y_n)$ be a random vector and define a statistical model $\{f_{\mathbf{Y}}(\mathbf{y}|\theta) : \theta \in \Theta\}$ which is parametrized by $\theta = (\theta_1, ..., \theta_n)$, the parameter vector in the parameter space $\Theta$. The likelihood function is the mapping defined as $L : \Theta \to [0, 1] \subset \mathbb{R}$ given by equation 8.2.

$$L(\theta|\mathbf{y}) = f_{\mathbf{Y}}(\mathbf{y}|\theta) \tag{8.2}$$

In other words, the likelihood function is functionally the same in form as a probability density function (pdf). However, the emphasis is changed from $\mathbf{y}$ to $\theta$. The pdf is a function of the $\mathbf{y}$'s while holding the parameters $\theta$'s constant, $L$ is a function of the parameters $\theta$'s, while holding the $\mathbf{y}$'s constant. We can abbreviate $L(\theta|\mathbf{y})$ to $L(\theta)$. The parameter vector $\hat{\theta}$ such that $L(\hat{\theta}) \geq L(\theta)$ for all $\theta \in \Theta$ is called maximum likelihood estimate, or MLE, of $\theta$. Many of the density functions are exponential in nature, therefore it is easier to compute the MLE of a likelihood function $L$ by finding the maximum of the natural log of $L$, known as the log-likelihood function defined in equation 8.3 due to the monotonicity of the log function. Finding maximum of a function is carried by taking the first derivative of that function and finding the values of parameters which equate the derivative to zero.

$$\ell(\theta|\mathbf{y}) = \ln(L(\theta|\mathbf{y})) \tag{8.3}$$

## 8.3 Derivation of Log-likelihood Function for SARMA Model

We begin the derivation by choosing a SARMA model that is described by equation 8.4.

$$\mathbf{y} = \rho\mathbf{W}\mathbf{y} + \mathbf{x}\beta + \mathbf{u}$$
$$\mathbf{u} = \delta\mathbf{W}\mathbf{u} + \varepsilon \tag{8.4}$$

We can explicitly write SARMA(1,1) model using its matrix-vector form in equation 8.4 as follows:

$$y_t = (\mathbf{I} - \rho\mathbf{W})^{-1}(x_{t1}\beta_1 + x_{t2}\beta_2 + ... + x_{tk}\beta_k + u_t)$$
$$u_t = (\mathbf{I} - \delta\mathbf{W})^{-1}\varepsilon_t \tag{8.5}$$

where $t = 1, ..., n$ is the index for $n$ succesive observations. Let us assume that the disturbances or error $\varepsilon_t$ is distributed normally, independently and identically with mean $E(\varepsilon) = 0$ and variance $\sigma^2$. The set of $n$ such equations can be compiled as equation 8.4. Let us assume that the disturbances $\varepsilon_t$, which are the elements of the vector $\varepsilon = [\varepsilon_1, ..., \varepsilon_t, ..., \varepsilon_n]$ and are distributed independently and identically according to a normal distribution defined in equation 8.6. Let's call the matrix $(\mathbf{I} - \rho\mathbf{W})$ as matrix $\mathbf{A}$ and the matrix $(\mathbf{I} - \delta\mathbf{W})$ as matrix $\mathbf{B}$ to simplify the expressions. Please note that $\varepsilon_t = (\mathbf{B}\mathbf{A}y_t - \mathbf{B}x_t.\beta)$.

$$N(\varepsilon_t; 0, \sigma^2) = \frac{1}{\sqrt{2\pi\sigma^2}} \exp\left(\frac{-1}{2\sigma^2}(\mathbf{B}\mathbf{A}y_t - \mathbf{B}x_t.\beta)\right) \tag{8.6}$$

If the vector $\varepsilon$ has a multi-variate normal distribution just like in our case, the normal distribution is then defined in equation 8.7 with a covariance matrix defined as $\Sigma = \sigma^2 \mathbf{I}$. Please note that $|\Sigma|^{\frac{-1}{2}} = \sigma^n$, $\Sigma^{-1} = \frac{1}{\sigma^2}\mathbf{I}$ and $|\Sigma| = |\sigma^2 \mathbf{I}| = \sigma^{2n}$.

$$N(\varepsilon_t; 0, \Sigma^2) = (2\pi)^{\frac{-n}{2}}|\Sigma|^{\frac{-1}{2}} \exp\left(\frac{-1}{2}\varepsilon_t^T \Sigma^{-1}\varepsilon_t\right)$$

$$= (2\pi)^{\frac{-n}{2}}|\Sigma|^{\frac{-1}{2}} \exp\left(\frac{-1}{2}(\mathbf{BA}y_t - \mathbf{B}x_{t.}\beta)^T \, \Sigma^{-1}(\mathbf{BA}y_t - \mathbf{B}x_{t.}\beta)\right)$$

$$(8.7)$$

Then, taking the $x_{t.}$ vectors which forms the rectangular matrix $\mathbf{x}$ of size $n$-by-$k$ as data, the observations $y_t$ (where $t = 1, ..., n$) have density functions $N(y_t; (\mathbf{BA}y_t - \mathbf{B}x_{t.}\beta), \sigma^2)$ which are of the same form as those of the disturbances, and the likelihood function of $\beta$ and $\sigma^2$, based on sample is defined in equation 8.8 [28]. Thus, the prediction of the SAR and SARMA model solutions heavily depend on the quality of the normally distributed random numbers generated.

$$L(\theta|\mathbf{y}) = L((\rho, \delta, \beta, \sigma^2)|(y_t, x_{t.}, \mathbf{W})) = \prod_{t=1}^{n} N(y_t; (\mathbf{BA}y_t - \mathbf{B}x_{t.}\beta), \sigma^2)$$

$$= N(\varepsilon; 0, \Sigma^2)|d\varepsilon/d\mathbf{y}|$$

$$= (2\pi)^{\frac{-n}{2}}|\Sigma|^{\frac{-1}{2}} \exp\left(\frac{-1}{2}(\mathbf{BA}y - \mathbf{B}x\beta)^T \, \Sigma^{-1}(\mathbf{BA}y - \mathbf{B}x\beta)\right) |d\varepsilon/d\mathbf{y}|$$

$$= (2\pi\sigma^2)^{\frac{-n}{2}} \exp\left(\frac{-1}{2}(\mathbf{BA}y - \mathbf{B}x\beta)^T \, \Sigma^{-1}(\mathbf{BA}y - \mathbf{B}x\beta)\right) |d\varepsilon/d\mathbf{y}| \quad (8.8)$$

The *Jacobian* term $|d\varepsilon/d\mathbf{y}|$ [19, 22] needs to be calculated out in order to find the probability density function of the variable $\mathbf{y}$, which is given by equation 8.9. Please note that $\varepsilon = (\mathbf{BA}y - \mathbf{B}x\beta)$ and the term $\Sigma^{\frac{-1}{2}}(\mathbf{BA}y - \mathbf{B}\beta)$ is also known as the vector of homoskedastic random disturbances [62]. The Jacobian term is equal to the identity matrix $\mathbf{I}$ in classical linear regression model [2]. The need for the Jacobian term is formally stated and proved by Theorem 7.1 (Theorem 2.1 in this paper) on pages 232-233 of [22]. We provide the theorem and proof for the reader's convenience by converting to our notation.

$$|d\varepsilon/d\mathbf{y}| = |\mathbf{BA}| = |\mathbf{B}||\mathbf{A}| \quad (8.9)$$

Applying Theorem 2.1, we can proceed as follows. Let $N(\varepsilon; 0, \Sigma^2)$ be the value of the probability density of the continuous random variable $\varepsilon$ at $\varepsilon_t$. Since the function given by $\mathbf{y} = \mathbf{A}^{-1}\mathbf{x}\beta + \mathbf{A}^{-1}\mathbf{B}^{-1}\varepsilon$ is differentiable and either increasing or decreasing for all values within the range of $\varepsilon$ for which $N(\varepsilon; 0, \Sigma^2) \neq 0$, then for these values of $\varepsilon$, the equation $\mathbf{y} = \mathbf{A}^{-1}\mathbf{x}\beta + \mathbf{A}^{-1}\mathbf{B}^{-1}\varepsilon$ can be uniquely solved for $\varepsilon$ to give $\varepsilon = \mathbf{BA}y - \mathbf{B}x\beta$ and the probability density of $\mathbf{y}$ is given by:

$$L(\theta|\mathbf{y}) = N(\varepsilon; 0, \Sigma^2)|d\varepsilon/d\mathbf{y}| \text{ provided } \mathbf{A}^{-1}\mathbf{x}\,\beta + \mathbf{A}^{-1}\mathbf{B}^{-1}\varepsilon \neq 0 \quad (8.10)$$

Elsewhere, $L(\theta|\mathbf{y}) = 0$.

$$
\begin{aligned}
L(\theta|\mathbf{y}) &= (2\pi\sigma^2)^{-\frac{n}{2}} \exp\left(\frac{-1}{2\sigma^2}(\mathbf{BAy} - \mathbf{Bx}\beta)^T (\mathbf{BAy} - \mathbf{Bx}\beta)\right) |\mathbf{BA}| \\
&= (2\pi\sigma^2)^{-\frac{n}{2}} \exp\left(\frac{-1}{2\sigma^2}(\mathbf{Ay} - \mathbf{x}\beta)^T \mathbf{B}^T \mathbf{B}(\mathbf{Ay} - \mathbf{x}\beta)\right) |\mathbf{BA}|
\end{aligned}
$$

(8.11)

$L(\theta|\mathbf{y})$ shown in equation 8.11 will henceforth be referred to as the "likelihood function of the SARMA(1,1) model". It is a probability distribution but now interpreted as a distribution of parameters which have to be calculated as noted in the Section 8.2. Since the log function is monotonic and the log-likelihood function is uni-modular , we can then equivalently minimize the log-likelihood function, which has a simpler form and can handle large numbers. This is because the logarithm is advantageous, since $\ln(ABC) = \ln(A) + \ln(B) + \ln(C)$. After taking the natural logarithm of equation 8.11, we get the log-likelihood function (equation 8.12).

$$
\begin{aligned}
\ell(\theta|\mathbf{y}) = \ln L(\theta|\mathbf{y}) = &-\frac{n}{2}\ln(2\pi) - \frac{n}{2}\ln(\sigma^2) - \\
&\frac{1}{2\sigma^2}(\mathbf{Ay} - \mathbf{x}\beta)^T \mathbf{B}^T \mathbf{B}(\mathbf{Ay} - \mathbf{x}\beta) + \ln|\mathbf{B}| + \ln|\mathbf{A}|
\end{aligned}
$$

(8.12)

The MLE estimators in equations 8.13a and 8.13b are obtained by setting $\frac{\partial \ell(\theta|\mathbf{y})}{\partial \beta}$ and $\frac{\partial \ell(\theta|\mathbf{y})}{\partial \sigma^2}$ to zero respectively.

$$
\hat{\beta} = ((\mathbf{Bx})^T (\mathbf{Bx}))^{-1}(\mathbf{Bx})^T \mathbf{BAy}
$$

(8.13a)

$$
\hat{\sigma}^2 =
$$
$$
(\mathbf{Ay})^T (\mathbf{I} - \mathbf{x}((\mathbf{Bx})^T (\mathbf{Bx}))^{-1} (\mathbf{Bx})^T \mathbf{B})^T \mathbf{B}^T \mathbf{B}(\mathbf{I} - \mathbf{x}((\mathbf{Bx})^T (\mathbf{Bx}))^{-1} (\mathbf{Bx})^T \mathbf{B})(\mathbf{Ay})
$$

(8.13b)

Replacing $\hat{\beta}$ given by equation 8.13a with $\beta$ in equation 8.12 and $\hat{\sigma}^2$ given by equation 8.13b with $\sigma^2$ in equation 8.12 lead to equation 8.14 for the log-likelihood function (i.e. the logarithm of the ML function) to be optimized for $\rho$.

$$\ell(\theta|\mathbf{y}) = \underbrace{\ln|\mathbf{B}| + \ln|\mathbf{A}|}_{log-dets} - \underbrace{\frac{n}{2}\ln(2\pi) - \frac{n}{2}\ln\left\{\frac{1}{n}\right\} - \frac{1}{2n}}_{constants} -$$

$$\underbrace{\frac{n}{2}\ln(\mathbf{Ay})^T(\mathbf{I} - \mathbf{x}((\mathbf{Bx})^T(\mathbf{Bx}))^{-1}(\mathbf{Bx})^T\mathbf{B})^T\mathbf{B}^T\mathbf{B}(\mathbf{I} - \mathbf{x}((\mathbf{Bx})^T(\mathbf{Bx}))^{-1}(\mathbf{Bx})^T\mathbf{B})(\mathbf{Ay})}_{SSE}$$

$$(8.14)$$

The first two terms of equation 8.14, i.e., the log-dets, are nothing but the logarithm of the sum of a collection of scalar values including all of the eigen-values of the neighborhood matrix $\mathbf{W}$ as shown by equations 8.15a and 8.15b.

$$|\mathbf{I} - \rho\mathbf{W}| = \prod_{i=1}^{n}(1 - \rho\lambda_i) \rightarrow \ln|\mathbf{I} - \rho\mathbf{W}| = \sum_{i=1}^{n}\ln(1 - \rho\lambda_i) \qquad (8.15a)$$

$$|\mathbf{I} - \delta\mathbf{W}| = \prod_{i=1}^{n}(1 - \delta\lambda_i) \rightarrow \ln|\mathbf{I} - \delta\mathbf{W}| = \sum_{i=1}^{n}\ln(1 - \delta\lambda_i) \qquad (8.15b)$$

Hence, equation 8.16 gives the final form of the concentrated log-likelihood function after ignoring constant terms in equation 8.14 and then multiplying the resulting equation with the constant $\frac{-2}{n}$.

$$\min_{|\rho|<1;|\delta|<1} \frac{-2}{n}\ln|\mathbf{B}| - \frac{2}{n}\ln|\mathbf{A}| +$$

$$\ln(\mathbf{Ay})^T(\mathbf{I} - \mathbf{x}((\mathbf{Bx})^T(\mathbf{Bx}))^{-1}(\mathbf{Bx})^T\mathbf{B})^T\mathbf{B}^T\mathbf{B}(\mathbf{I} - \mathbf{x}((\mathbf{Bx})^T(\mathbf{Bx}))^{-1}(\mathbf{Bx})^T\mathbf{B})(\mathbf{Ay})$$

$$(8.16)$$

Therefore, the concentrated log-likelihood function optimized using multi-variable optimization routine quasi-Newton (in *fmincon* of Matlab) to find the best estimates for $\rho$ (and $\delta$) Once the estimates for $\rho$ (and $\delta$) is found, both $\beta$ and $\sigma^2$ can be computed.

## 8.4  Proof for Eigen-values of Markov Matrix which are bounded in $[-1,+1]$ and occur in $\pm$ pairs

**Proof:** Let $\lambda = max_i(\lambda_i)$, and $\lambda_{min} = min_i(\lambda_i)$. By the Perron-Frobenius theorem (please see page 32 of [6] and page 120 of [17]), $\lambda_i \geq -\lambda$. As $\mathbf{W}$ is row-stochastic, we have $\lambda = 1$ (See §5.13.3 in [42]). The following argument clearly proves this fact. Suppose that $\lambda \in C$ is an eigen-value of $\mathbf{W}$ matrix and $\mathbf{X} \in V_n(C)$ is a corresponding eigen-vector. Then:

$$\mathbf{WX} = \lambda\mathbf{X} \qquad (8.17)$$

Let $k$ be such that $abs(x_j) \leq abs(x_k), \forall j, 1 \leq j \leq n$. Then, equating the $k^{th}$ component of each side of equation 8.17 gives:

$$\sum_{j=1}^{n} w_{kj} x_j = \lambda x_k \qquad (8.18)$$

Hence:

$$abs\,(\lambda x_k) = abs(\lambda)abs(x_k) = abs\left(\sum_{j=1}^{n} w_{kj} x_j\right)$$

$$\leq \sum_{j=1}^{n} w_{kj} abs(x_j) \leq \sum_{j=1}^{n} w_{kj} abs(x_k) = abs(x_k) \qquad (8.19)$$

Hence $abs(\lambda) \leq 1$. This is the first part of the proof which says that the eigenvalues of a Markov matrix are smaller than 1.

Now, we deal with the second part of the proof: Since the $\lambda_i$ are real, and all roots of modulus $\lambda$ differ (See page 120 of [17]), there can be at most two $\lambda_i$ of modulus $\lambda$. For sites on a uniform grid, returns to a site can occur merely after an even number of steps. In other words, let's consider a symmetric non-row-stochastic matrix like matrix $\mathbf{C}$ or a non-sysmmetric row-stochastic matrix $\mathbf{W}$ derived from the graph (as suggested by the Perron-Frobenius theorem). Figures 8.1(a), 8.1(b), 8.1(c) and 8.1(d) prove lemma 2.1, where B denotes black node and R denotes red node in the grid.

| 1R | 2B | 3R | 4B |
|----|----|----|----|
| 5B | 6R | 7B | 8R |
| 9R | 10B | 11R | 12B |
| 13B | 14R | 15B | 16R |

(a) The spatial framework visualized as chess-board, which is $\phi$-by-$q$ where $\phi$ may or may not be equal to $q$.

| 1R | 9R | 2B | 10B |
|----|----|----|-----|
| 11R | 3R | 12B | 4B |
| 5B | 13B | 6R | 14R |
| 15B | 7B | 16R | 8R |

(b) The reordered spatial framework where we gather black nodes and red nodes together.

$$\begin{bmatrix} 0 & \mathbf{A} \\ \mathbf{B} & 0 \end{bmatrix}$$

(c) The corresponding adjacency-like matrix structure

$$\begin{bmatrix} 0 & \mathbf{A} \\ \mathbf{B} & 0 \end{bmatrix}\begin{bmatrix} \mathbf{u} \\ \mathbf{v} \end{bmatrix} = \lambda \begin{bmatrix} \mathbf{u} \\ \mathbf{v} \end{bmatrix} \quad and \quad \begin{bmatrix} 0 & \mathbf{A} \\ \mathbf{B} & 0 \end{bmatrix}\begin{bmatrix} \mathbf{u} \\ -\mathbf{v} \end{bmatrix} = -\lambda \begin{bmatrix} \mathbf{u} \\ -\mathbf{v} \end{bmatrix}$$

(d) Eigen-values of both non-row-stochastic and row-stochastic neighborhood matrices occur in $\pm$ pairs and $\mathbf{u}, \mathbf{v}$ are any two vectors

**Fig. 8.1** Proving the lemma 2.1 where B denotes black node and R denotes red node in the grid.

First, let's color them as a chess board into two colors such as red and black as shown in Figure 8.1(a). The neighbors for every red node should be all black, and vice versa. Then, we order all the red nodes first, then all the black nodes as shown in Figure 8.1(b). Then the corresponding adjacency-like (neighborhood) matrix will look like the structure as shown in Figure 8.1(c) (because no red node is directly connected to another red node, and vice versa.)

As a special case, we have $\mathbf{B} = \mathbf{A}^T$ if binary neighborhood matrix $\mathbf{C}$ is used. This is shown in Figure 8.1(d), where we prove that any matrix of the form shown in Figure 8.1(c) has eigen-values in plus-minus ($\pm$) pairs (except for the zero eigen-values). This means for a row-stochastic $\mathbf{W}$ that all sites have period of two. Thus, $\lambda_{min} = -\lambda_i$ and the eigen-values occur in pairs such as $\pm\lambda_i$. This completes the proof. A similar proof can be found on page 192 of [43]. $\square$

## 8.5 Basic Linear Algebra Facts

The basic linear algebra equalities [11] used in our proofs are following.

- A real $n$-by-$n$ matrix $\mathbf{A}$ is called a Markov matrix, or row-stochastic matrix if:
  1. $a_{ij} \geq 0$ for $1 \leq i, j \leq n$;
  2. $\sum_{j=1}^{n} a_{ij} = 1$ for $1 \leq i \leq n$.
- If $\mathbf{A}$ is a Markov matrix, then $\mathbf{AJ}_n = \mathbf{J}_n$ where $\mathbf{J}_n = [1, ..., 1]^T$. So, 1 is always an eigen-value of a Markov matrix.
- If $\mathbf{A}$ and $\mathbf{B}$ are Markov matrices, then $\mathbf{AB}$ is also a Markov matrix.
- $tr(\mathbf{A} + \mathbf{B}) = tr(\mathbf{A}) + tr(\mathbf{B})$
- $tr(\mathbf{AB}) = tr(\mathbf{BA})$
- Length of any $n$-by-1 vector $\mathbf{x}$ is equal to $\sum_{i=1}^{n} x_i^2$
- $\sum_{i=1}^{n} \lambda_i = tr(\mathbf{A})$ and $\prod_{i=1}^{n} \lambda_i = |\mathbf{A}|$
- $tr(\mathbf{A}) = \sum_{i=1}^{n} a_{ii}$
- If the square of an idempotent matrix $\mathbf{A}$ is non-singular, then that matrix is the identity matrix. Because: $\mathbf{A}^2 = \mathbf{A}$ then $\mathbf{A}^{-1}\mathbf{A}^2 = \mathbf{A}^{-1}\mathbf{A}$ which means $\mathbf{A} = \mathbf{I}$.
- All idempotent matrices have roots of only 0 or/and 1.
- If $\mathbf{A}$ is positive definite (or positive semi-definite) matrix and $\mathbf{B}$ is non-singular matrix i.e., its determinant is not zero then $\mathbf{B}^T\mathbf{AB}$ is also positive definite (or positive semi-definite) matrix [11].
- All orthogonal matrices have real roots as $\pm1$
- All positive definite matrices are non-singular.
- $tr(k\mathbf{A}) = k\, tr(\mathbf{A})$ where $k$ is a scalar.
- Latent toots of positive semi-definite matrices are non-negative.
- For a symmetric matrix $\mathbf{A}$ we have $\mathbf{A} = \mathbf{A}^T$.
- If:
  1. $\mathbf{x}^T\mathbf{Ax} > 0$ then the matrix $\mathbf{A}$ is called positive definite matrix $\forall \mathbf{x} \neq 0$.
  2. $\mathbf{x}^T\mathbf{Ax} \geq 0$ then the matrix $\mathbf{A}$ is called positive semi-definite matrix $\forall \mathbf{x}$.

- All idempotent matrices are positive semi-definite with non-negative digonal elements since $\mathbf{A}^T\mathbf{A} = \mathbf{A} \wedge \mathbf{A}^T = \mathbf{A} = \mathbf{A}^2$. Then, $\mathbf{x}^T\mathbf{A}\mathbf{x} = (\mathbf{A}\mathbf{x})^T\mathbf{A}\mathbf{x}$ which is just a sum of squares of the elements of $\mathbf{A}\mathbf{x}$.
- The determinant of an orthogonal matrix is equal to 1 or $-1$.
- Orthonormal vector is a vector that is both orthogonal and normalized (i.e., length is 1).
- Please note that the matrix $\mathbf{M}$ corresponds to the symmetric and idempotent matrix $\mathbf{x}(\mathbf{x}^T\mathbf{x})^{-1}\mathbf{x}^T$. The matrix $(\mathbf{I} - \mathbf{M})$ is also idempotent because $(\mathbf{I} - \mathbf{M})(\mathbf{I} - \mathbf{M}) = \mathbf{I}^2 - 2\mathbf{M} + \mathbf{M}^2 = \mathbf{I} - 2\mathbf{M} + \mathbf{M} = (\mathbf{I} - \mathbf{M})$. On the other hand, $(\mathbf{I} - \mathbf{M})$ is also symmetric i.e., $(\mathbf{I} - \mathbf{M}) = (\mathbf{I} - \mathbf{M})^T$ because the negat ive sign in front of the matrix $\mathbf{M}$ does not change the symmetry property and since the identity matrix $\mathbf{I}$ just changes the diagonal elements by adding 1 to it, which also does not change the symmetry.

## 8.6 Proof of symmetry of $(\mathbf{I} - \rho\mathbf{W})^T(\mathbf{I} - \mathbf{M})(\mathbf{I} - \rho\mathbf{W})$

**Proof:** The matrix $\mathbf{M}$ corresponds to the symmetric and idempotent matrix $\mathbf{x}(\mathbf{x}^T\mathbf{x})^{-1}\mathbf{x}^T$. We also know that the matrix $(\mathbf{I} - \mathbf{M})$ is both idempotent and symmetric. That is why we have $(\mathbf{I} - \mathbf{M})^T(\mathbf{I} - \mathbf{M}) = (\mathbf{I} - \mathbf{M})$. Let's take the tranpose of $(\mathbf{I} - \rho\mathbf{W})^T(\mathbf{I} - \mathbf{M})(\mathbf{I} - \rho\mathbf{W})$:

$$
\begin{aligned}
((\mathbf{I} - \rho\mathbf{W})^T(\mathbf{I} - \mathbf{M})(\mathbf{I} - \rho\mathbf{W}))^T &= (\mathbf{I} - \rho\mathbf{W})^T(\mathbf{I} - \mathbf{M})^T(\mathbf{I} - \rho\mathbf{W}) \\
&= \underbrace{(\mathbf{I} - \rho\mathbf{W})^T(\mathbf{I} - \mathbf{M})(\mathbf{I} - \rho\mathbf{W})}_{\text{Arrived at the original matrix}} \quad (8.20)
\end{aligned}
$$

Thus, the matrix $(\mathbf{I} - \rho\mathbf{W})^T(\mathbf{I} - \mathbf{M})(\mathbf{I} - \rho\mathbf{W})$ is equal to its transpose which means it is a symmetric matrix. $\square$

## 8.7 Proof of $(\mathbf{I} - \rho\mathbf{W})^T(\mathbf{I} - \mathbf{M})(\mathbf{I} - \rho\mathbf{W}) \geq 0$

This proof is in other words for showing that the matrix $(\mathbf{I} - \rho\mathbf{W})^T(\mathbf{I} - \mathbf{M})(\mathbf{I} - \rho\mathbf{W})$ is positive semi-definite. **Proof:** We know that the matrix $(\mathbf{I} - \mathbf{M})$ is both idempotent and symmetric and it is positive semi-definite and the matrix $(\mathbf{I} - \rho\mathbf{W})$ is non-singular. We also have the following fact: If $\mathbf{A}$ is positive definite (or positive semi-definite) and $\mathbf{B}$ is non-singular i.e., its determinant is not zero then $\mathbf{B}^T\mathbf{A}\mathbf{B}$ is also positive definite (or positive semi-definite) [11]. Thus, our matrix $(\mathbf{I} - \rho\mathbf{W})^T(\mathbf{I} - \mathbf{M})(\mathbf{I} - \rho\mathbf{W})$ is positive semi-definite. $\square$

## 8.8 Single Variable Optimization: The Golden Section Search

We use the Golden Section Search (GSS) algorithm in the single-variable optimization process of our SAR model solutions which covers multi-dimensional spaces. To the best of our knowledge only one study [40] used this algorithm for the same purpose but in only one dimesional space. Figure 8.2 presents the pseudocode for the GSS algorithm [24].

---

**Algorithm 8.8.1:** THE GOLDEN SECTION SEARCH$(a, b, c, xmin, tol, f)$

$g \leftarrow 1.0 - 0.61803399$
$x0 \leftarrow a$
$x3 \leftarrow c$
**comment:** we have intervals $(a, b)$ and $(b, c)$

**if** $(b, c)_{right-interval} > (a, b)_{left-interval}$

 **then** $\begin{cases} \textbf{comment: } \text{split right interval to get the new intervals as follows} \\ (a, b)(b + g * (c - b), c) \\ x0 \leftarrow a; x1 \leftarrow b; x2 \leftarrow b + g * (c - b); x3 \leftarrow c \end{cases}$

 **else** $\begin{cases} \textbf{comment: } \text{split left interval to get the new intervals as follows} \\ (a, b - g * (b - a))(b, c) \\ x0 \leftarrow a; x1 \leftarrow b - g * (b - a); x2 \leftarrow b; x3 \leftarrow c \end{cases}$

$f1 \leftarrow f(x1)$
$f2 \leftarrow f(x2)$
**while** $(x3 - x0)_{interval} > tol * (abs(x1) + abs(x2))$

 **do** $\begin{cases} \textbf{if } (f2 < f1) \\ \quad \textbf{then} \begin{cases} \textbf{comment: } \text{drop left value} \\ x0 \leftarrow x1; x1 \leftarrow x2; \\ \textbf{comment: } \text{split right interval} \\ x2 \leftarrow r * x1 + g * x3; \\ f1 \leftarrow f2; f2 \leftarrow f(x2) \end{cases} \\ \quad \textbf{else} \begin{cases} \textbf{comment: } \text{drop right value} \\ x3 \leftarrow x2; x2 \leftarrow x1; \\ \textbf{comment: } \text{split left interval} \\ x1 \leftarrow r * x2 + g * x0; \\ f2 \leftarrow f1; f1 \leftarrow f(x1) \end{cases} \end{cases}$

**if** $(f1 < f2)$
 **then** $xmin \leftarrow x1;$
 **else** $xmin \leftarrow x2;$
**return** $(xmin)$

---

**Fig. 8.2** The pseudo-code of the GSS Algorithm

The *tol* in the program corresponds to the upper bound for the relative error of *xmin*. We would expect a termination condition like $|xmin - b| < tol * |b|$. However the exact value $b$ of the minimum is unknown. Assume that $x1$ will be chosen as *xmin*. (If $x2$ will be chosen as *xmin*, the situation is symmetric.) Then we know that $b$ is in the interval $[x0, x2]$ and hence that $|xmin - b| = |x1 - b| <= max(|x1 - x0|, |x2 - x1|) = |x1 - x0| < |x3 - x0|/2$. If the termination condition of the program is satisfied, then it follows that $|xmin - b| < tol * (|x1| + |x2|)/2$ and $(|x1| + |x2|)/2$ is approximately equal to $|b|$. The choice of *tol* is left to the user. As explained in the text, its order of magnitude should be the square root of the machine precision. So if the machine precision is $10^{-8}$ (and if we have no a priori information about the function itself $f(b)$ and its second derivative $f''(b)$) then we should set *tol* to about $10^{-4}$.

## 8.9 Multi-variable Search

We used Matlab's *fmincon* which is a constrained multi-variable search when we estimated SARMA(1,1) model parameters $\rho$ and $\delta$. It uses Quasi-Newton optimization algorithm for medium sized problems.

# References

1. E. Anderson, Z. Bai, C. Bischof, S. Blackford, J. Demmel, J. Dongarra, J. D. Croz, S. H. A. Greenbaum, A. McKenney, and D. Sorensen. Lapack user's guide. *Society for Industrial and Applied Mathematics*, 1999.
2. L. Anselin. *Spatial Econometrics: Methods and Models*. Kluwer Academic Publishers, Dordrecht, 1988.
3. Z. Bai and G. Golub. Some unusual matrix eigenvalue problems. *Proceedings of VECPAR'98 - Third International Conference for Vector and Parallel Processing*, 1573:4–19, 1999.
4. R. Barry and R. Pace. Monte carlo estimates of the log-determinant of large sparse matrices. *Linear Algebra and its Applications*, 289:41–54, 1999.
5. F. Bavaud. Models for spatial weights: A systematic look. *Geographical Analysis*, 30:153–171, 1998.
6. A. Berman and R. Plemmons. *Nonnegative Matrices in the Mathematical Sciences*. Computer Science and Applied Mathematics, 1979.
7. J. Besag. Spatial interaction and the statistical analysis of lattice systems. *Journal of the Royal Statistical Society, B*, 36:192–225, 1974.
8. J. Besag. Statistical analysis of nonlattice data. *The Statistician*, 24:179–195, 1975.
9. L. Blackford, J. Choi, A. Cleary, E. D'Azevedo, J. Demmel, I. Dhillon, J. Dongarra, G. H. S. Hammarling, A. Petitet, K. Stanley, D. Walker, and R. Whaley. Scala-pack user's guide. *Society for Industrial and Applied Mathematics*, 1997.
10. B. Boots and A.Getis. *Point Pattern Analysis*. SAGE Publications, 1988.
11. E. Borghers and P. Wessa. Scientific resources. *http://www.xycoon.com/matrix-algebra.htm*.
12. M. Celik, B. M. Kazar, S. Shekhar, D. Boley, and D. J. Lilja. Spatial dependency modeling using spatial auto-regression. *In Proc. of the ISPRS/ICA Workshop on Geospatial Analysis and Modeling as part of Int?l Conference GICON*, 2006.
13. R. Chandra, L. Dagum, D. Kohr, D. Maydan, J. McDonald, and R. Menon. *Parallel Programming in OpenMP*. Morgan Kauffman Publishers, 2001.
14. S. Chawla, S. Shekhar, W. Wu, and U. Ozesmi. Modeling spatial dependencies for mining geospatial data. *1st SIAM International Conference on Data Mining*, 2001.
15. W. Cheney and D. Kincaid. *Numerical Mathematics and Computing*. 1999.
16. T. M. Corp. Cmssl for cm-fortran: Cm-5 edition. *Cambridge*, 1993.
17. D. Cox and H. Miller. *The Theory of stochastic processes*. Methuen, London, 1965.
18. N. Cressie. *Statistics for Spatial Data*. Wiley, New York, 1993.
19. R. Davidson and J. MacKinnon. *Estimation and Inference in Econometrics*. Oxford University Press, New York, 1993.
20. J. W. Demmel. *Applied Numerical Linear Algebra*. SIAM, 1997.
21. J. Dongarra. Information about freely available eigenvalue-solver software. *http://www.netlib.org/utk/people/JackDongarra/la-sw.html*.
22. J. Freund and R. Walpole. *Mathematical Statistics*. Prentice Hall, 1980.
23. G. Golub and C. V. Loan. *Matrix Computations*. Johns Hopkins University Press, 1996.
24. G. Gonnet. Scientific computation. *http://linneus20.ethz.ch:8080/faq/faq.jsp*, 2002.
25. D. Griffith. *Advanced Spatial Statistics*. Kluwer Academic Publishers, 1998.
26. D. A. Griffith. Faster maximum likelihood estimation of very large spatial autoregressive models: An extension of the Smirnov-Anselin result. *Journal of Statistical Computation and Simulation*, 74(12):855–866, 2004.
27. N. A. Group. Nag smp fortran library. 2004.
28. F. Hayashi. *Econometrics*. Princeton University Press, 2000.
29. R. Horn and C. Johnson. *Matrix Analysis*. Cambridge University Press, 1985.
30. R. Horn and C. Johnson. *Topics in Matrix Analysis*. Cambridge University Press, 1994.
31. B. Kazar, S. Shekhar, and D. Lilja. Parallel formulation of spatial auto-regression. *AHPCRC Technical Report No: 2003-125*, 2003.
32. B. Kazar, S. Shekhar, D. Lilja, and D. Boley. A parallel formulation of the spatial auto-regression model for mining large geo-spatial datasets. *SIAM International Conf. on Data Mining Workshop on High Performance and Distributed Mining (HPDM2004)*, April 2004.

33. B. Kazar, S. Shekhar, D. Lilja, D. Boley, D. Shires, J. Rogers, and M. Celik. A parallel forumulation of the spatial autoregression model. *GISPlanet: II International Conference and Exhibition on Geographic Information*, 2005.

34. B. Kazar, S. Shekhar, D. Lilja, R. Vatsavai, and R. Pace. Comparing exact and approximate spatial auto-regression model solutions for spatial data analysis. *Third International Conference on Geographic Information Science (GIScience2004)*, October 2004.

35. B. Klinkenberg. Geography 471: Applied gis: Using your knowledge. *http://www.geog.ubc.ca/courses/geog471/notes/*.

36. J. LeSage. Econometrics toolbox for matlab. *http://www.spatial-econometrics.com/*.

37. J. LeSage. Solving large-scale spatial autoregressive models. *Second Workshop on Mining Scientific Datasets*, 2000.

38. J. LeSage and R. Pace. Using matrix exponentials to explore spatial structure in regression relationships (bayesian mess). *http://www.spatial-statistics.com*, 2000.

39. J. P. Lesage and R. K. Pace. *Introduction to Spatial Econometrics*. Champman and Hall/CRC, 2009.

40. B. Li. Implementing spatial statistics on parallel computers. *Practical Handbook of Spatial Statistics, CRC Press*, pages 107–148, 1996.

41. D. Long. Spatial autoregression modeling of site-sepecific wheat yield. *Geoderma*, 85:181–197, 1998.

42. M. Marcus and H. Minc. *A Survey of Matrix Theory and Matrix Inequalities*. Dover, New York, 1992.

43. R. Martin. Approximations to the determinant term in gaussian maximum likelihood estimation of some spatial models. *Statistical Theory Models*, 22(1):189–205, 1993.

44. J. Mathews. Proof for chebyshev polynomial approximation. *http://math.fullerton.edu/mathews/n2003/ChebyshevPolyProof.html*, 2003.

45. B. Novosadov and V.V.Zhogina. A method of calculating eigenvectors of real symmetric tridiagonal martices in a hyperspherical space. *International Journal of Chemistry*, 42:819–826, 1992.

46. L. E. A. Oleg A. Smirnov. An O(N) parallel method of computing the log-jacobian of the variable transformation for models with spatial interaction on a lattice. *Computational Statistics & Data Analysis*, 53(8):2980–2988, 2009.

47. J. Ord. Estimation methods for models of spatial interaction. *Journal of the American Statistical Association*, 70:120–126, 1975.

48. Y. Oykov, O. Veksler, and R. Zabih. Fast approximate energy minimization via graph cuts. *International Conference on Computer Vision*, 1999.

49. R. Pace and R. Barry. Quick computation of spatial auto-regressive estimators. *Geo-graphical Analysis*, 29:232–246, 1997.

50. R. Pace and J. LeSage. Closed-form maximum likelihood estimates for spatial problems (mess). *http://www.spatial-statistics.com*, 2000.

51. R. Pace and J. LeSage. Semiparametric maximum likelihood estimates of spatial dependence. *Geographical Analysis*, 34(1):76–90, 2002.

52. R. Pace and J. LeSage. Simple bounds for difficult spatial likelihood problems. *http://www.spatial-statistics.com*, 2003.

53. R. Pace and J. LeSage. Spatial auto-regressive local estimation (sale). *Spatial Statistics and Spatial Econometrics, ed. by Art Getis*, 2003.

54. R. Pace and J. LeSage. Chebyshev approximation of log-determinant of spatial weight matrices. *Computational Statistics and Data Analysis*, 2004.

55. R. Pace and D. Zou. Closed-form maximum likelihood estimates of nearest neighbor spatial dependence. *Geographical Analysis*, 32(2), 2000.

56. W. Press, S. Teukulsky, W. Vetterling, and B. Flannery. *Numerical Recipes in Fortran 77*. Cambridge University Press, 1992.

57. S. Shekhar and S. Chawla. *Spatial Databases: A Tour*. Prentice Hall, 2003.

58. S. Shekhar, B. Kazar, and D. Lilja. Scalable parallel approximate formulations of multi-dimensional spatial auto-regression models for spatial data mining. *24th Army Science Conference*, November 2004.

59. S. Shekhar, P. Schrater, R. Raju, and W. Wu. Spatial contextual classification and prediction models for mining geospatial data. *IEEE Transactions on Multimedia*, 4(2):174–188, 2002.

60. O. A. Smirnov and L. E. Anselin. Fast maximum likelihood estimation of very large spatial autoregressive models: A characteristics polynomial approach. *Computational Statistics and Data Analysis*, 35(3):301–319, 2001.

61. J. Timlin, C. Walthall, Y. Pachepsky, W. Dulaney, and C. Daughtry. Spatial regression of crop parameters with airborne spectral imagery. *3rd Int. Conference on Geospatial Information in Agriculture and Forestry*, 2001.

62. R. van der Kruk. A general spatial arma model: Theory and application. *ERSA (Europian Regional Science Association) Conference*, pages 110–131, 2002.